THE COLORED ATLAS OF LOVEBIRDS

***AGAPORNIS:* more than a hobby, a passion!**

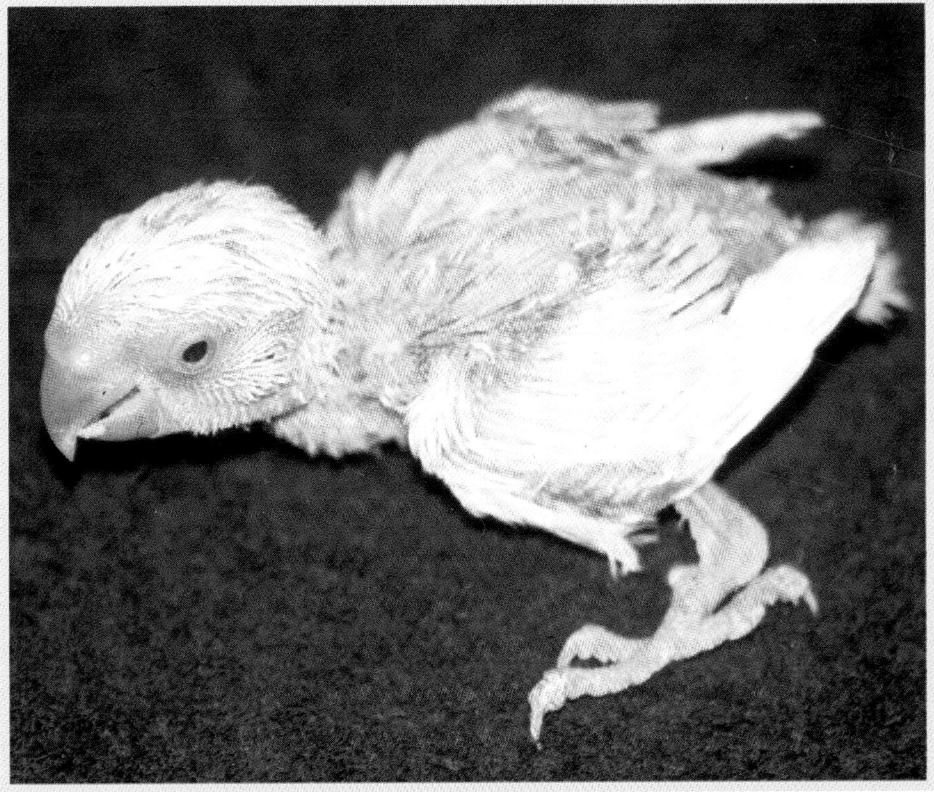

Whiteface American Yellow *roseicollis*, three weeks old. Note the frilled plumage, thin legs, and a head disproportionately large relative to the rest of the body—these are signs of malnutrition. In this case the problem was chronic diarrhea.

DRAWINGS:
DR. ROSSANO D'ANGIERI

AUTHOR:
DR. ALESSANDRO D'ANGIERI.

Terms used in this work to identify plumage and external features of *Agapornis* and their mutations.

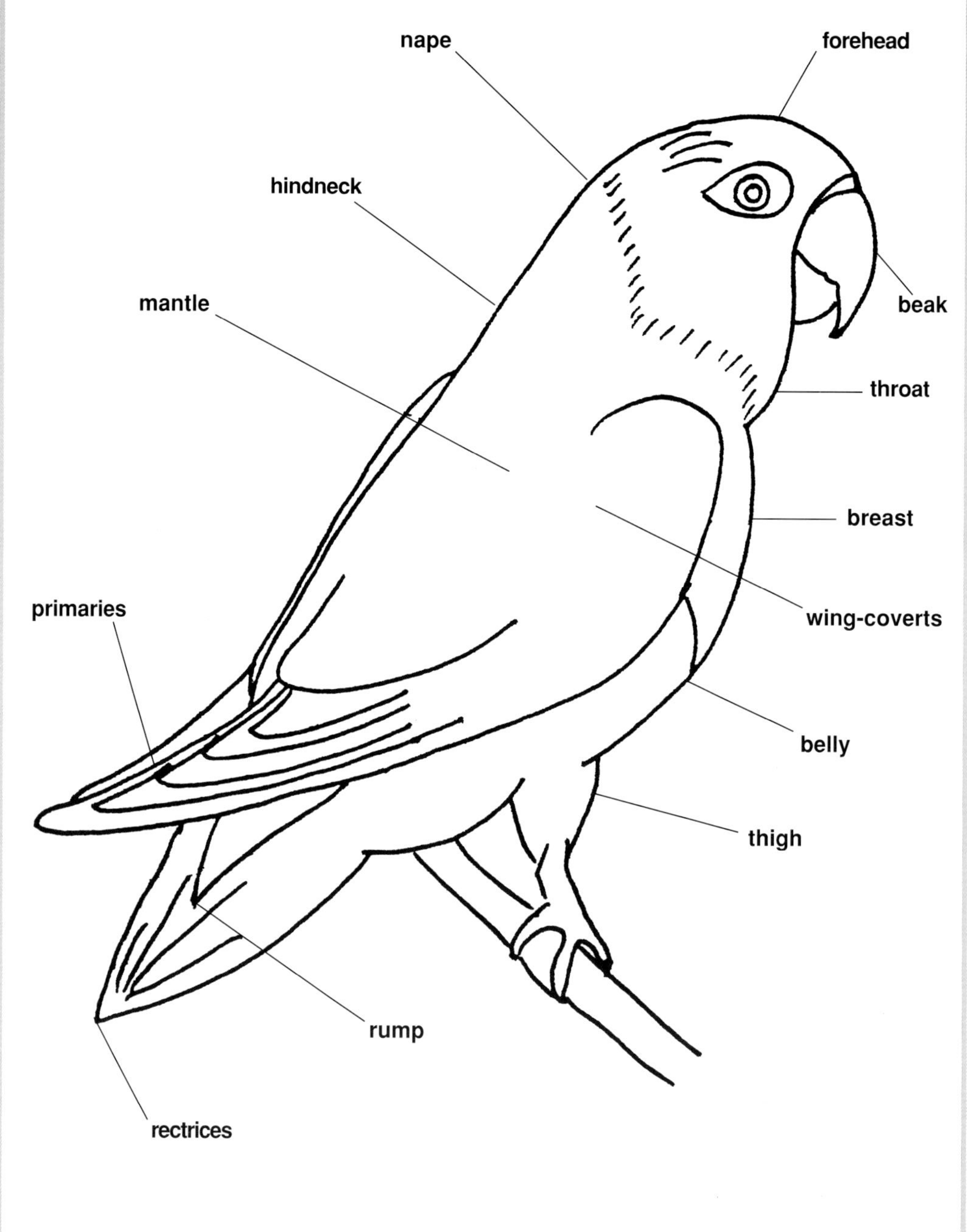

CONTENTS

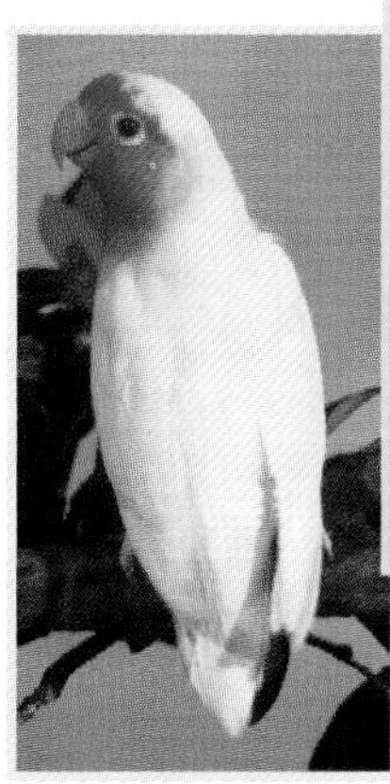

ABOUT THE AUTHOR—

Dr. Alessandro D'Angieri, who was born in Brazil, is a physician, amateur ornithologist, and collaborative researcher in the State University of Campinas's Zoology Department (UNICAMP). He dedicates his life to the preservation and study of Brazilian and foreign birds. He works mainly in the area of behavioral and genetic studies and has published several articles on these topics.

When he was eighteen years old, he received the "Ordem do Conde do Parnaíba," a local prize for those who are devoted to the sciences; he has also been honored twice by the Brazilian Society for Scientific Progress (SBPC), at two national congresses.

Dr. D'Angieri is an aviculturist who has bred ornamental birds since childhood. He is also chairman of the Brazilian chapter of the World Pheasant Association, an international body promoting galliform preservation worldwide.

He has dedicated the last sixteen years to lovebird breeding, studying the mutations and developing combinations. He has attained an eminent position in Brazilian "agapornism" and is an active member in breeders associations in the USA, Germany, England, and Australia, where he has published articles on lovebirds, contributing in this way to the development of the agapornism in the world!

DEDICATION

To that one who taught me to love and preserve the animals and all of Nature; who showed me the importance of the birds to the environment and of aviculture to bird preservation, this same aviculture into which I was introduced by him early on.

To that one who taught me the techniques and secrets of bird breeding and showed me the paths of science so that I could continue upon them.

To one of the pioneers of Brazilian lovebird breeding whose dedication in a short while achieved for us a prominent position in both Brazilian and world agapornism and made the realization of this work possible.

I dedicate this book to my father, Dr. Attílio Nelson D'Angieri, whose moral support was, is, and will always be fundamental. Thank you very much, Dad!"

ACKNOWLEDGMENTS

I am grateful to all my lovebird-breeding colleagues who have allowed their birds to be photographed, and to all those people who have contributed in some way to the elaboration and conclusion of this work.

I specially thank Mr. Renato Bizzan, owner of IMAGEM photo laboratories, who is always ready to process my films immediately, which facilitated the preparation of this book. His advice is always helpful.

I would like to thank specially the following people (in alphabetical order): Mr. Dagoberto Azzoni; Mr. Duvílio Baldan; Mrs. Adriana D'Angieri; Miss Rosana D'Angieri; Dr. Rossano D'Angieri; Prof. Dr. Esleib Ghion; Mr. José Herculano Gouveia; Mr. Roy Hevesi; Mr. Johan Kloosterman; Mr. Luigi Mamprim; Mr. Mitsutoshi Nakandakare; Mr. José Maria Fusca Neto (in memoriam); Mr. Luiz Mauro Oliveira; Mr. Marcos Antonio Pechir; Mr. Roberto Ervino Raffell; Miss Elisángela Fátima Sampaio; Prof. Washington Simões; Mr. Nigel Steele-Boyce; Mr. Howard K. Swann (in memoriam); Mr. Fabio Tiezzi; Prof. Dr. Jacques M. E. Vielliard; Mr. Gerrit Voz; Prof. Sérgio S. Zavan; Mr. Bernd Ziegenfuss.

The author is open to all comments, criticisms and suggestions that can lead to the improvement of this work and the hobby and science of *Agapornis* breeding. You can contact the author by writing to: Dr. Alessandro D'Angieri, Rua Barão do Rio Branco 253, CEP 13201-670, Jundiaí-SP, Brazil. Phone/ FAX (11) 437-5403.

American Pied *roseicollis*. This is a heavily pied Peach-faced Lovebird. The American Pied factor characteristically shows the rose mask sharply demarcated from the upper breast.

PREFACE

Parrot breeding has been widespread in the world for a long time. The Australian Budgerigars (*Melopsittacus undulatus*) were the first to be bred in captivity: it was 1840 when John Gould introduced them to England, and even today the English Budgerigar is a model famed worldwide.

Early in this century Imperialism and the conquest of the African continent provided the occasion that introduced a new parrot group to European aviculture. These miniature parrots were well adapted to captivity. Their behavior was very singular: the little parrots were always in pairs together, caressing each other; this behavior earned them the English appellation "lovebirds."! In France they were called *les inséparables* and in Germany *Unzertrennlichen*, both meaning "the inseparables."

They came from Africa to Brazil at the end of the 1950s. Very little was known about their habits and behavior, and for years they were called "African parraquets."

In the sixties they were widely bred in Europe and in America, and these strange creatures, neither parakeets nor parrots, became widespread and mutations appeared. Their genus name, *Agapornis*, started to be used more often; etymologically it too (*agape*, love; *ornis*, bird) means "lovebird."

Agapornis breeding in Brazil developed in the seventies and was largely established in the eighties. Goals appeared among the breeders: to get new colors, to select bloodlines, and to make contact with other breeders around the world. "Agapornism" was created—this neologism certainly won't be found in the dictionaries, but it subsumes *per se* all this admiration and dedication to the breeding of those "little African parrots" which we with love call *agapornis*, the same birds that have enchanted many people and have been gaining ground among breeders and families as pets worldwide.

The lack of specialized literature that can satisfy the emerging need for information by both beginners and veterans in agapornism has motivated us to compose this work.

We will try in this book to use simple language, at the same time being as complete as possible, making it accessible to the beginners and interesting to the most experienced. It is however far from being a totally complete work; that would be impossible due to the immensity of the subjects involved. Thus our main focus will be genetics, but we will try to be as encompassing as possible.

We invite you now, dear reader, to come with us into this fascinating world of agapornism that is, without doubt, much more than a hobby: *it's a passion!*

Agapornis genus distribution in
AFRICAN CONTINENT

- *Agapornis cana*
- *Agapornis pullaria*
- *Agapornis roseicollis*
- *Agapornis p. fischeri*
- *Agapornis p. lilianae*
- *Agapornis taranta*
- *Agapornis swinderniana*
- *Agapornis p. personata*
- *Agapornis p. nigrigenis*

THE GENUS *AGAPORNIS*

The birds of the genus *Agapornis* (Selby) are represented by nine distinct forms in the wild, all from continental Africa, except *Agapornis cana* (Gmelin), which is found on the island of Madagascar. The agapornis belong to the order Psittaciformes, family Psittacidae, and subfamily Psittacinae, encompassing about 262 species and 63 genera. In Brazilian territory, all the native psittacines (70 species, 18 genera) are from the subfamily Psittacinae.

Following is a list of the nine principal *Agapornis* forms:

• *Agapornis cana* (Gmelin). Habitat: littoral border of Madagascar.

• *Agapornis pullaria* (Linné). Habitat: Central Africa, from Guinea to Lake Victoria and the islands of San Tomé and Principé.

• *Agapornis taranta* (Stanley). Habitat: highlands of Ethiopia.

• *Agapornis swinderniana* (Kuhl). Habitat: forested areas of West and Central Africa.

• *Agapornis roseicollis* (Vieillot). Habitat: southwestern Africa.

• *Agapornis personata fischeri* Reichenow. Habitat: northern Tanzania to the south of Lake Victoria.

• *Agapornis personata personata* Reichenow. Habitat: northeastern Tanzania, from Lake Manyara to the Iringa Highlands.

• *Agapornis personata lilianae* Shelly. Habitat: southern

Fallow *fischeri*. This newest Australian mutation is called Avocado. Photo courtesy of *Australian Birdkeeper Magazine* and Mr. Roy Havesi.

Apple Green *roseicollis*. This coloration is the expression of the Whiteface and Pastel factors in a double heterozygote (split) condition.

Medium Green *personata*. This is a Green which was darkened by the addition of one Dark factor.

***Agapornis personata nigrigenis*. Wild coloration. A small head and beak are characteristic of pureness.**

Tanzania, northwestern Mozambique to southern Malawi, throughout eastern Zambia and the Zambesi River Valley.

• *Agapornis personata nigrigenis* Sclater. Habitat: confined to southwestern Zambia in the Zambesi River Valley.

Additionally, in the case of *cana, pullaria, swinderniana,* and *roseicollis*, subspecies which are not very greatly distinct from one another have been described.

The above species can be divided into three evolutionary groups: two distinct and one intermediate (Moreau 1948; Dilger 1960). The *cana-pullaria-taranta* group is the most primitive; it shows sexual dimorphism in all three species. Females are totally green except in *pullaria*, in which females have a duller orange on the forehead. The nests are structurally simple.

The intermediate *roseicollis-swinderniana* group shows no sexual dimorphism and exhibits a more elaborate nest construction. It is important to state that we have no data on *swinderniana* nests due to its unsuitability to captivity and no evidence from the wild so far.

The *personata* group (authorities differ on allowing these forms specific or subspecific status) is the most evolved of all, due to a complex social and nesting behavior that we will see in the following chapters.

Pied Dark Pastel (Pied Mauve) *roseicollis*. A combination of the American Pied factor, homozygous Dark factor, and the Pastel factor.

Danish Violet Medium Green (Violet Jade) *roseicollis*. Note the results of the violet shade on the green. It is darker than with just the Dark factor alone. The rump is a deep violet blue color. (Single Violet factor).

Pied American Yellow *roseicollis*. In this case a suffusion of the yellow pied markings occurred producing a homogeneous bright gold color. This is certainly one of the most beautiful combinations in the *Agapornis* species. Note the rump slightly tinged with blue, a characteristic of the American Yellow factor.

Medium Green (Jade) *roseicollis*. Note the darkening of the body's green and the rump's blue colors.

AGAPORNIS BEHAVIOR

Pied Dark Green American Cinnamon (Pied Cinnamon Olive, or American Pied Mustard) *roseicollis*. Note the gray rump, which is characteristic of double Dark-factored birds.

Medium Apple Green *roseicollis*. Here there are three factors involved: Dark factor, Whiteface factor, and Pastel factor—a triple heterozygote bird.

We will try to present in a general way some behavioral patterns related to the reproduction, social organization, and genetics of the *agapornis*. It would be impossible to cover every subject, so we have restricted this chapter to the main points which are interesting to aviculturists as well as ethologists. It is important to state that the reported behaviors are the same with respect to mutations and subspecies, with exceptions noted as needed.

PAIR FORMATION

The birds start the search for a partner when still very young, in many instances, when they are still begging the parents for food. In the *A. personata* forms, this begins about 16–18 days after leaving the nest; in *A. roseicollis* this bonding will occur a little bit later, generally when the young start losing the characteristic black color in the beak (very visible in the wild phenotype), which occurs 28–32 days after fledging. *A. cana*, *A. pullaria*, and *A. taranta* will form pairs just after their fourth month of life, as the primary social unit consists of the pair and their young (Dilger 1960). The formation of a pair is accomplished similarly in all *Agapornis* forms: the birds start searching for one another, getting closer, and then try to caress each other.

The mutual caressing consists only of feather preening; no sexual approach is observed. This will occur by the third or fourth month of life in *roseicollis, personata,* and *fischeri*; the sixth or seventh month in *cana, pullaria,* and *taranta*; and between the fourteenth and eighteenth month in *lilianae* and *nigrigenis.*

When the young are in flocks, thcy can try scvcral timcs with different birds before choosing a definite partner. Once together, the pair will remain so for life—except when several attempts at reproduction are fruitless or if we force the pairing. With forced pair formation a certain tolerance seems to occur; the pair will breed, but not as successfully as natural (non-forced) pairs. Offered an opportunity to make different choices, a forced pair can "divorce," and new pairs can be easily formed. We can also observe that if we separate a naturally formed pair, the birds will have difficulty pairing with other birds.

It is observed that in colonies of several birds, including different species, there will be a preference for birds of the same species and parental color. If this option is not available, there is a preference scale: first will come conspecific mutations. Among the mutations, the preference is clearly for birds of parental color. Thus females will mate more frequently with males that have their father's phenotype and the males with those which have their mother's phenotype.

Two birds of different species have great difficultly forming

Dark Green (Olive) *roseicollis.* This is the result of two Dark factors on the wild (green) ground color.

Whiteface Cobalt *roseicollis.* A single Dark factor on a Whiteface ground color.

pairs, just as though we forced the union. There is an exception when the individuals are raised by foster parents; for example, a *personata* raised by a *roseicollis* will see the latter as its own species.

After pair formation, or "marriage," male and female can always be seen together, justifying in this way the name *lovebird.*

The naturally formed pairs will be good breeders, but often, in order to get new genetic combinations, we need to dictate the matings!

HOMOSEXUALITY

When individuals of the opposite sex are lacking, occasionally pairing between two individuals of the same sex (males or females) may occur; in general, such a union is dissolved as soon as an individual of the opposite sex becomes available. But it is not rare that, after a long period of "homosexual" relationship, the members will not accept an individual of the opposite sex.

The mature homosexual pair can exhibit a behavior very similar to heterosexual pairs. In a pair consisting of two adult males, attempts at copulation may be undertaken by either bird. Mutual courtship feeding is also observed, and a rudimentary nest is built.

A two-female pair also will attempt copulation, nest building, and courtship feeding. These behaviors so closely simulate a true pairing that the birds will be confirmed as two females only after eggs appear: eight or more eggs will be laid. In general, both females will incubate the eggs, but it is possible that only one of the females will, while the other assumes the male role, feeding "his" female in the nest. When the incubation period ends, there won't be any chicks, of course. A resting period of two or three weeks follows, and then another reproductive cycle begins.

This homosexuality has been observed only in *Agapornis personata* and *A. roseicollis*; so far we know no instances in the other lovebird species.

SEXUAL APPRENTICESHIP

In all *Agapornis* species one can observe a total lack of sexual experience in young birds, mainly the males. The young males are totally inexperienced in their

Orangeface *roseicollis.* The psittacin dilution occurs over the bird's entire body.

A lightly Pied Dark Pastel American Cinnamon (Pied Cinnamon Mauve) *roseicollis*. The gray rump is characteristic of double Dark-factored birds.

attempts, and so are frequently rejected by the females. One can observe young males trying mount the females the wrong way around; the females, when such faulty attempts occur, become quite aggressive and disturbed. After several such attempts the males become frustrated by the rejection but never give up. This frustration is demonstrated in the more primitive species by scratching the head feathers. This behavior lost its meaning in the other species, and can even be a sign of exhibitionism and ostentation, which is a more complex ethological pattern.

After several attempts, the males will gain experience and each time will copulate more correctly; the rejections by the females will decrease.

The young females do not exhibit a similar ineptitude; they appear able to copulate correctly without any need to learn from successive attempts.

CONQUEST AND DEFENSE OF TERRITORY

As soon as a young true pair (male and female) reach sexual maturity, they can be observed searching for a nesting site, a nest

Medium Green American Cinnamon (Jade Cinnamon) *roseicollis*.

box in this case. When kept in colonies, the territorial distribution occurs without problems and with no peculiarities most of the time; each pair will choose a nest box as its territory.

When nests are not available in sufficient numbers or when two or more pairs choose the same nest box, there may be squabbles among the contenders for the nest. In these cases, the females are the most aggressive ones. This "combat" generally is limited to feet banging and beak shaking (as a duel). The loser will abandon the territory. Progressively, all territories are occupied.

Medium Green American Cinnamon (Jade Cinnamon) *roseicollis.*

When one of the combatants does not give way, violent duels may occur. Birds may be mortally wounded (mainly in *Agapornis personata personata* and *A. p. fischeri*).

The pair's territory is limited to the nest box and adjacent perches. A fledgling will be tolerated only in the vicinity of its own parents' territory (they promptly recognize the youngster as theirs). It will be rejected and expelled from the territories of others. The young birds won't offer any resistance to leaving the "foreign" territories, often flying to other foreign territory and so on, finally returning to the protection of their own parents' territory or to a neutral one. *Agapornis cana*, *A. pullaria*, and *A. taranta* offer exceptions; in these species the young will defend territory aggressively, together their parents.

When a new individual of a different species (*agapornis* or not) is introduced into a colony, it will be attacked at once by all or some members of the colony and may even be torn to pieces if not promptly removed from the aviary. This fact was observed by me several times, and once it happened in an *Agapornis p. fischeri* colony with a Chinese Francolin (*Francolin pintadeanus*, a member of the pheasant family and essentially a ground-dwelling bird). It was introduced into the *fischeri* aviary, supposing that there would be no harassment of a bird that lives on the ground (supposedly neutral territory). What I observed was a terrible attack on the little partridge; as soon as I distanced myself from the aviary, all the colony flew onto the Francolin on the ground. Although it was promptly taken out, unfortunately it was severely wounded. It's likely that events like this would not occur in the wild, because there the *agapornis* feed on trees where food can be found. In captivity the food is placed on the ground, so the lovebirds may consider the ground as part of their ecological niche.

NEST BUILDING

All the *Agapornis* forms do build nests, although in different types and shapes which are similar among conspecifics and their mutations.

In captivity all *agapornis* (except *pullaria*) will build nests with straw and leaves. Some aviculturists use palm leaves to get the birds to build the nests.

Agapornis cana and *A. taranta* carry the straw and other nesting material inserted in their plumage and build a very simple nest amounting to just a covering on the nest floor.

Agapornis pullaria are exceptional, they carry some nesting material. They do not breed in captivity not as readily as the other lovebirds. In the wild, *pullaria* nest in hollows dug in arboreal termitaria, or sometimes in terrestrial ones. Some breeders will construct an artificial termitarium and offer it to the birds to excavate their own nests. The most practical and efficient way to breed *pullaria* successfully is to offer traditional nest boxes filled with a solid block of cork. The birds can make their own nest and thus will be more stimulated to breed.

The *roseicollis* are on a higher evolutionary level and build a more elaborate nest: inside the nest box in a cuplike shape divided in two "rooms." The first is small and leads to a second, larger chamber, where the eggs are laid and incubated. The nesting material is mostly transported inserted in the plumage; occasionally it is carried in the beak to the nest entrance, where it is tucked into the feathers and carried into the nest. This behavior is an example of the evolutionary transition to *personata*.

A heavily Pied Medium Green American Cinnamon (Pied Jade Cinnamon) *roseicollis*.

Nesting behavior is different in *personata.* The individuals will transport nesting material only in the beak and ninety percent of the time will do it after several stops on nearby perches. The twigs carried are in general very large, permitting construction of a more elaborate nest inside the nest box. They build a double-decker nest: the very small upper chamber is linked to the lower room by a vertical cylindrical tube—often a short spiral—about 4 cm in diameter. The lower space, which contains the eggs, is larger, and generally the birds close the "corridor" between it and the upper room.

Medium Pastel (Cobalt Pastel) *roseicollis.* This bird is merely a Pastel with one Dark factor.

In all lovebird species both male and female participate in nest construction. The females work more intensively, mainly in the more primitive species.

It is important to note that young pairs are not able to build very elaborate nests. Theirs are more simple than the nests of older pairs. With each succeeding reproductive cycle, a pair will improve their nest-building technique. Generally, three cycles are needed to gain enough experience to build a nest like a practiced breeding pair.

HYBRIDIZATION

Hybridization must be avoided by aviculturists, and the pure forms must be preserved—especially among the *personata* group, in which hybrids will be fertile, as we will see shortly. Dilger produced hybrids between *roseicollis* and *fischeri,* and out of curiosity the author decided to do the same. These birds behave similarly to their parents, but when they start to build their nest for the first time the birds are quite confused about how to do it and try alternately to transport the nest material in the feathers and in the beak. They put the twigs in their plumage and take it out almost immediately. After a period of about three or four months the birds finally decide to transport the nesting material in the beak and become successful in nest construction (the nest is similar to that of *roseicollis*). These hybrids are in truth "mules"; they always prove to be infertile but are excellent foster parents.

COURTSHIP FEEDING

This can be observed during the building of the nest and throughout the reproductive cycle: the birds feed each other. The male, after emitting some sharp sounds, goes toward the female, shaking his head in oscillatory movements, at the same time regurgitating food as a visual stimulus. The female accepts the food and also feeds the male back. In the primitive group (*cana, pullaria,* and *taranta*), courtship feeding is done only by the males, and frequently copulation will follow.

COPULATION

Copulation, both in the more primitive and in the more evolved *agapornis*, occurs on the nest box in ninety percent of the cases (except for young pairs occasionally seen copulating on the ground); the remaining ten percent will occur on perches after solicitation by the female. It is common for a pair to always copulate in the same place. We call the aviculturist's attention to the importance of not removing nest boxes from the cages and aviaries.

Copulation occurs three to five times a day, lasting from six to ten minutes. It usually takes place between 10 A.M. and 1 P.M. and between 5 and 6 P.M. It may occasionally occur outside these periods. Generally, copulation starts two weeks before the first egg is laid and continues until the last is laid. It is also common to observe the entire colony copulating at the same time.

INCUBATION AND EGGS

The first egg is laid about two weeks after copulation starts. One

Whiteface American Cinnamon *roseicollis.*

egg is laid every other day, resulting in three to five. Seven-egg clutches have been observed by the author in *roseicollis*. Nests with eight or more eggs must be suspected of being used by two females (in a colony), or the "pair" may consist of two females. Although there are records of a ten-egg clutch in *cana* and a fifteen-egg clutch in *pullaria* (Schönwetter 1964), we believe these may be an accumulation of clutches, not single clutches.

Incubation begins after the third egg is laid, and 22–23 days later the first chick will be born (the incubation period is valid for all species). In a brood, it is common to observe a large difference in the chicks' sizes, due to the hatching intervals from the first and last egg. It takes the chick about forty-eight hours to break out of the shell.

During incubation, females leave the nest two or three times a day, at which times they usually will be treaded by their males. After the last egg is laid, the females will leave the nest more rarely, and they are fed in the nest by the males. Often they won't stay out of the nest for more than seven or eight minutes. But on very warm days it is common to observe the females outside for longer periods, probably in order to avoid overheating.

Danish Violet Medium American Cinnamon (Violet Jade American Cinnamon) *roseicollis*. This bird has just one Dark factor and one Violet factor on a Cinnamon Green ground color. Note the general darkening of the plumage. The rump assumes a lilac shade.

THE YOUNG

At hatching, the chicks are about 1.5–2.0 cm long and covered with a sparse down, which varies in color according to the species and the mutation.

In one week they will double in size, and another week later will have doubled once more. About the second week their eyes start to open, and the first feather sheaths are visible. At about four weeks of age they will be almost completely feathered. When six weeks old, they will leave the nest for the first time (seven weeks in *taranta*). By the tenth week they will be totally independent.

It is quite common, mainly in *personata*, if nesting material or food is insufficient, for the females to pluck the youngsters' feathers out, causing serious wounds. This can also occur when the parents want to start a new breeding cycle and the young are still in the nest.

The female stays in nest during the first two weeks of the chicks' life. After this time it is usual to see her outside for longer periods. Once the young are feathered, she will stay in the nest only at night.

In the first days of life, the food brought by the male will be enough to feed all the chicks; but gradually it will become necessary for the female also to go out for food. The male will begin to feed the young directly when the chicks are about two weeks old. If it happens, as was once observed, that the female dies before they are two weeks old, the male won't be able to feed them. If the male dies, the female will continue to feed the chicks but will have difficulty getting enough food into them to rear them to maturity. Generally, only the stronger and older ones will survive.

At about four weeks of age, the young are completely feathered and start to "take a look" outside the nest. Often, the parents will close the nest entrance with nesting material in order to prevent the premature exit of the young. This behavior seems to be a parental way of controlling precipitate excursions by the young, until they have grown enough to open the nest "door" by themselves and will certainly be more able to face life outside the nest.

On the average, the young are fed about three times a day and will be under their parents' protection for about another thirty days more. During this period the young spend the great majority of their time on the nest box or on the ground trying to learn to feed by themselves, once the parents decline to feed them. The parents can be observed offering seeds to the young, instead of regurgitating the food. This may be a teaching behavior to induce the young to learn to feed.

When about sixty days old, the young won't be tolerated by parents any longer and will be expelled from the territory.

NEW PAIRS IN A BREEDING COLONY

When a new pair is introduced into a breeding colony, it will be promptly rejected and seen as enemies even when in neutral territory. If the new pair is strong enough, they can establish their

A heavily Pied Dark American White (Pied Silver Cherry Mauve) *roseicollis*. Here you see four factors combined: American Pied (single factor), American Yellow, Pastel, and Dark (double factor). The Mendelian probability of obtaining this bird is 3.125%.

Dark Pastel (Mauve) *roseicollis*. Here two dark factors are added to a Pastel bird.

problems in trying to make other pairings with the "divorced" birds, unless they had not paired naturally. It will take some weeks before the birds will accept a new mate. This period is about as long as the time they were together.

It is possible that the birds will never mate with different birds, particularly if they experienced long periods (years) of successful breeding cycles together. On the other hand, a recently formed pair, which have not reared a brood, can be separated reasonably easily and will more readily accept other birds as mates.

Spontaneous separation can be observed with pairs that have experienced several fruitless breeding attempts. These naturally "divorced" birds will search for other mates; this is a notable example of species preservation.

There are records of fifteen-year-old pairs that are still active and breeding in captivity.

own territory, but it will be very difficult, due to the owners' hostility.

On the other hand, if a pair is taken out of the colony, the other members will emit loud sounds and fly nervously by the wire and even try to follow the removed birds. If this pair are reintroduced days or even weeks later, they will be recognized by the colony and promptly accepted.

SEPARATING A PAIR

When a pair is split up in order to manipulate crossings and matings, there may be

Opposite: Apple Green American Cinnamon *roseicollis*. This is an American Cinnamon bird split for both Whiteface and Pastel factors.

BREEDING IN CAPTIVITY

Nowadays, without doubt, *agapornis* are in a top position in world aviculture, maybe just below budgerigars and canaries. All species in the genus, except *Agapornis swinderniana*, have adapted very well to captivity, but the most popular is the Peach-faced Lovebird, *Agapornis roseicollis*. *Roseicollis* is at the top of agapornism, about fifty times more common than those in second place: the *personata* forms. This ranking seems to be similar on every continent. The other species may be more or less common in different countries, but overall they can be considered rare. The predominance of *roseicollis* is due to several factors: they reach sexual maturity earlier; they can be bought more cheaply; they are easier to mate; they are healthier, more robust, and better adapted to captivity; their general care is easier; they nest even in poor conditions, without proper nesting material; juveniles are resistant to sickness and can withstand adverse climates.

IMPORTANT NOTE: We do not want to discourage the aviculturist from keeping the less familiar lovebird species! It can be said that in general, all of them breed quite well. We just want to call your attention to some peculiarities in the breeding techniques. Pay attention to each rule, and you will not have insurmountable problems with *pullaria* any more than with *roseicollis*. We do, however, advise the beginner to start with Peach-face Lovebirds and to acquire the other species after getting some experience.

About *personata* we can say that: their nesting and aviary requirements are more exacting; they won't breed without proper nesting material; they are more expensive; they can be paired less easily than *roseicollis*—sometimes is very difficult to find compatible birds; they are quite aggressive, which makes for difficult keeping and colony formation; the males particularly are more susceptible to stress and sicknesses, which leads to a larger number of females reaching adult age.

About *cana*, *pullaria* and *taranta*: they are rarer and much more expensive; they are quite aggressive and generally must be housed in single pairs; they reach sexual maturity much later than the others; they are shy and therefore need a quiet and calm situation. *Pullaria* are very stressable birds and require special nests (containing cork, for example).

Opposite: Lutino *personata*. Note the red eye, characteristic of Ino-factor homozygosity.

Blue (right) and Cobalt on left (blue plus one Dark factor) *A.p.personata.*

REPRODUCTION

In captivity breeding takes place the year around; at any time you can have success with lovebirds. There is a break only during molting, which will occur around the end of the summer or the beginning of autumn. There are on the average about four clutches a year.

Several aviculturists advise allowing the birds only two reproductive cycles a year, in order to prevent overworking and stressing the birds. However, in the author's experience, problems will occur whenever the birds are poorly kept, with respect to conditions, aviaries, or food, or if birds are mated when still too young. But well-nourished pairs of sufficient age will breed without problems four times a year.

The ideal maturity for mating birds would be as follows (species, age in months): *roseicollis*, 10; *lilianae*, 18–24; *nigrigenis*, 18–24; *personata*, 12–14; *fischeri*, 10–14; *pullaria*, 12–16; *cana*, 12–16; *taranta*, 10–16; *swinderniana*, unknown. Of course, there may be instances of earlier or later maturity.

Every two years, we advise you to take the nest boxes out of the aviaries or cages for a six-to-eight-month resting period. This way you will be preventing stress and certainly will have good breeding pairs for eight to twelve years.

WHERE AND HOW TO BREED

We must have our main objectives in mind before starting to breed lovebirds.

There are basically two ways of breeding lovebirds: housed as single pairs or in colonies. Colonies have the advantage of being easier to manage. In just a single large aviary we can keep several pairs, managing all birds at the same time. The amount of work done for one pair will serve for all. And the overall prospect of a colony is very beautiful.

However, there are some disadvantages: The pairings are difficult to control, particularly if there are birds of the same phenotype in a colony. Genetic control is almost impossible because it is difficult to ascertain the parents of every youngster, and there is also the possibility that two females will lay eggs in the same nest. In the case of death, it can be difficult to tell which of the colony members is the survivor of the pair and what its sex is. Serious territorial fights may occur: many eggs and birds can be lost. There is a risk of epidemics in the case of infectious diseases. Juvenile mortality is higher due to fights and mutual aggressiveness. You may inadvertently remove a breeding bird instead of a youngster if the birds are not properly identified with rings.

HOW TO SET UP A BREEDING COLONY

A breeding colony cannot be easy to set up; you must follow some basic principles:

Cana, *pullaria*, and *taranta* do not adapt well to colonies. They will do well in large aviaries (at least two cubic meters per pair).

Paisagism can be successfully combined with agapornism. Here you see the author's aviaries.

The other species need about one cubic meter per pair.

All the birds that will be housed as a colony must be pair-bonded and be about the same age.

All the birds must be placed into the aviary at the same time, in order to reduce the severity of territorial disputes.

All birds must be ringed so that they can be distinguished from their youngsters easily.

The number of nest boxes must be equal to or greater than the number of females.

Enough nesting material for all pairs must be on hand.

Avoid placing perches very close to the nests.

Following these principles is essential; if you do, then you will not encounter many problems in keeping a colony successfully.

SINGLE-PAIR BREEDING

This method of breeding lovebirds can have some disadvantages if you have many pairs. The work of managing ten pairs will be ten times bigger than for a ten-pair colony, and the aviary cost will be much higher.

However, there are advantages: Quality and genetic control can be rigorous. Mortality rates due to fights will be zero. Infectious diseases are more easily controlled. You can increase the number of pairs as much as you like, without worrying about rejection by the colony. Single pairs can be kept in cages or small aviaries indoors or outdoors.

INDOORS VS. OUTDOORS

Though indoor breeding is quite common throughout the world, this situation is justified only in countries with too cold winters. *Agapornis* are very hardy birds and don't need to be kept indoors.

Although the advantages of protection and other practical aspects of care make indoor breeding appear preferable, observation shows that this is not totally correct. Indoor environments, with a very stable climate the year round, are a closed biological system. The birds will become very adapted to these conditions and to associated factors (diseases, for example).

In general, birds that are bred in such conditions will be more sensitive to any environmental variations that they may be exposed to.

We must bear in mind that not all other breeders will be able to provide the same environmental conditions that prevail in our aviaries; so it is quite common that indoor-bred birds cannot acclimate to different conditions and may be condemned to live with you forever.

On the other side, the outdoor-bred birds can escape easier, suffer predation, etc.

Lovebirds are very able to tolerate climatic variation and only require protection against rain and strong winds.

FOOD

Good food is essential for success with any bird species. A varied regimen of good food must be provided to the lovebirds in order to avoid malnourished young.

The staple foods offered daily should be seeds, greens, fruits, bread, and even milk. In particular these are: canary seed, wild chicory, Italian millet, cabbage, oats, bread, sunflower seed, rye bread, wheat, milky bread, barley, apple, green corn, and wild grasses. Several breeders recommend soybeans and sorghum (guinea corn) as supplementary foods, but in the author's experience such food is not very palatable to lovebirds.

Multivitamins should be given

White *personata*. This is the visual Dilute Blue split for Ino. The Ino and Dilute factors do interact, showing a snow white pattern. There is an increase in melanin dilution; the same can occur in the Green (non-Blue) series.

Dilute Dark Blue (Dilute Mauve) *personata*. The Dilute factor lightens the color pattern.

for three-to-five-day periods every two months and daily during stressful situations (molting, sicknesses, colder winters, etc.).

HOUSING

The most diverse kinds of housing can be used, depending on whether your objective is breeding or ornamentation. In the latter case, cages are more than enough and can be found in the most varied sizes and shapes.

We believe that your main purpose is to breed lovebirds. In this case it is more advisable to use small aviaries or big cages and to plan carefully where to build them.

Aviaries may be made of wood with wire netting as the front wall (half- or three-quarters-inch mesh). Small mesh-size is very important to prevent rodent attacks.

The enclosure size can vary according to your choice of breeding program: For single pairs, an aviary of at least 32 x 32 x 32 inches is advisable, constructed of wire netting; these can be set in racks. For colonies, just calculate to allow a minimum of one cubic meter of space for each pair (about 30 cubic feet).

Cobalt *personata*. The Dark factor on a true blue results in a bright, strong blue color. This is one of the most beautiful combinations in *personata* birds.

Nest box model used by the author.

NEST BOXES AND NESTING MATERIAL

Regarding nesting materials and nest-box models, the practices of breeders vary tremendously. The author's experience has been very successful and we believe that the models described will bring you the same success.

Nest boxes must be built of wood. We suggest wood 10 mm thick. It can be painted, but you should avoid light, clear color tones; dark brown or plum is advisable.

The measurements are 8.0 x 6.5 x 6.5 inches, with an entrance hole about 2.2 inches in diameter (1.8 inches for *nigrigenis*, *lilianae* and *cana*). A small perch below the entrance (about 4 inches long) is advisable. The nests for *pullaria* must be filled with solid cork; some European aviculturists use turf instead of cork, and clay can also be used with success.

The nesting material used by these little feathered engineers is in general straw or flexible twigs. Several kinds of straw can be used successfully since they provide enough strength to support the nest structure, yet don't present the danger of accidents such as hanging, etc. We suggest yellow broom straw. Some breeders use dry palm leaves or weeping-willow twigs.

EGGS AND CHICKS

A good breeding pair must lay eggs, incubate them, and raise the young properly.

Some care must be taken in

order to have better results with the clutches:

Nests must be inspected in order to check the number of eggs and approximate date they were laid. A second inspection must be done by the last egg's supposed hatching date in order to ascertain the number of hatched chicks; dead chicks and clear eggs must be removed.

To avoid damage to the embryos and subsequent losses, we should not make any inspection during the incubation period except for a pressing reason. After hatching, the nest's floor straw must be changed and cleaned weekly; this will decrease contamination and diseases.

Between the sixth and ninth days of the chicks' life they must be ringed and logged, recording their genotype and phenotype, along with the genotype and phenotype of their parents.

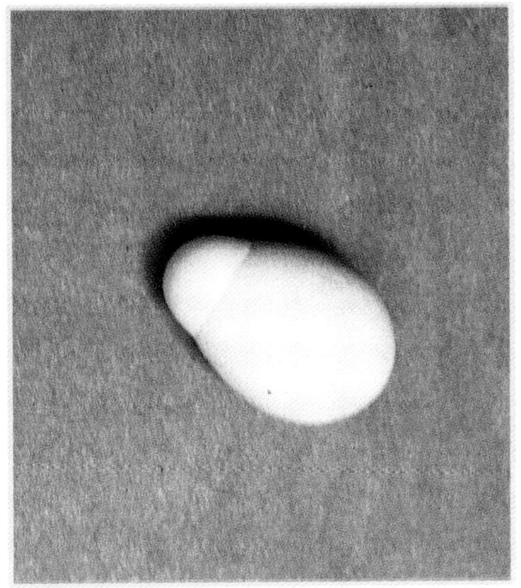

Over calcified egg. One cause of egg binding.

After the young have left the

Lovebird eggs in the nest.

nest, it must be dismantled. Fresh nesting material should be offered to the breeding pair so they can build a new, clean nest in time for the next clutch.

In the event of clear eggs or chicks dead-in-the-shell, you must verify if any of the following might have occurred and correct when necessary: overheating due to direct sunlight on the aviary or nest; lack of humidity in too dry climates; too much humidity; sterility of one or both parents; genetic incompatibility of the pair; chronic disease.

CONSANGUINITY

Consanguinity, the result of inbreeding, is a problem that must be faced by all fanciers of captive-animal breeding. Lovebird breeding is particularly subject to consanguineous mates, mainly when mutations and their combinations are involved. We can say that there are no mutant agapornids that don't have identical genes in their genetic makeup. In general, each mutant strain comes from a single bird, or very rarely two. All Lutinos, Cinnamons, etc. come from a single mutant bird which appeared one day and was selected.

In practice it is impossible to avoid consanguinity totally, but some basic principles should be followed:

You must always use healthy birds, ones not carrying any physical or behavioral defect that could be inherited by descendants. For example, a

Fallow *roseicollis* nestlings, two just hatched, the other a day old. Already at this time melanistic (black-eyed) birds can be distinguished from non-melanistic ones (red eyes).

Roseicollis chicks, 18 days old.

common mistake committed by aviculturists is to use females that don't rear their young as breeding females, giving their eggs to foster mothers for incubation. Proceeding this way will select for a "bad-breeder female" line. In our experience, the females produced from bad mothers will have a 57% greater chance of being a bad female; in some bloodlines it can reach 100%. This behavioral defect is certainly inherited and must be avoided, no matter how beautiful the chicks are.

Avoid as often as possible very closely related mates (father and daughter, brothers, etc.).

Always use pairs from distinct lineages: homozygous x heterozygous.

Introduce new blood lines as frequently as possible into your genetic breeding pool. Always try get birds of good provenance and quality. When in doubt, keep your breeding stock genetically closed (no outside birds).

If the above rules are strictly followed, you are going to get success in your breeding despite any consanguineous mates.

SEXING

Sex determination is one of the biggest problems in agapornism, as it is for any other breeder of species showing no sexual dimorphism.

Pied Danish Violet Medium Green *roseicollis*. Note the darkening produced by the violet shade on the green. Also, interaction with one Dark factor increases the darkening. This variety can be distinguished from a double Dark-factored one by its violet blue rump instead of the gray of the double Dark.

The techniques for sexing are numerous. Endoscopy is the fastest and most reliable, as it is done by experienced persons. Sexing is accomplished by direct visualization of the sex glands (testis and ovary) with a low possibility of error.

There are also laboratory tests based on cell cultures, karyotype, biochemical and immunological assays, and also radioimmunoassays and ELISA techniques.

All this technology is wonderful, but unhappily it is not always available promptly, at the right time and place. Thus, many times we are obliged to resort to a more archaic method, subject to errors, but which will in experienced hands be more than 90% trustworthy. We are talking about the digital palpation of the pelvic bones. The female agapornids have iliac bones longer and less curved than those of males. This enlarges the distance between the pelvic bones and between these and the posterior wall of the pelvis and external border. Males have more curved, shorter iliacs, which results in a short space between them and a very small pelvis.

The method consists of gentle palpation of the structures just mentioned, assessing the differences. Practice is fundamental; only after extensive training can you use digital palpation confidently. There are individual variations, especially related to age, which increases the incidence of error when sexing young birds. It might be said that you should palpate about a thousand birds to gain sufficient experience that you can trust it.

IDENTIFICATION OF MUTATIONS

With many of the *Agapornis* mutations, alterations to the color of the plumage and the soft parts are apparent from the moment the chicks hatch. By attending to the color of the eyes, beak, skin, and down feathers, the keen breeder can often tell whether any chicks of the the variety being bred for are contained in this brood. Also, if one is sure of the genetic makeup of the parents, with sex-linked mutations is can be possible to infer the sex of the chick.

Identification data for newborn chicks is summarized in Appendix 2, for both *roseicollis* and *personata* mutations.

Top: Red-suffused American Cinnamon *roseicollis* hen. The red suffusion can occur over the bird's entire body. Here you can see about 75% red suffusion.

Bottom: Back view of the same bird.

PIGMENTS AND PLUMAGE COLORATION

In general, avian coloration is derived from three kinds of pigments:

• Melanins: four types of melanin are known, but just two of these are important in the genus *Agapornis*: eumelanin (blackish) and phaeomelanin (brownish).

• Carotenoids: several kinds are known, from the basically red (erythrophylls) to the basically yellow (xanthophylls). These are very common in psittacines, which is why they are are popularly called *psittacins* in all parrotlike birds. These are some of the pigments that are responsible to the visible colors in *agapornis.*

• Porphyrins: produce some bright reds, yellows, and greens. It seems that the porphyrins aren't significant in *Agapornis* coloration.

The *Agapornis* colors are a consequence of the interaction of the effects of the melanins (eumelanin and phaeomelanin) with the carotenoids (psittacins), influenced by the feather structure, which produces the light-beam dispersion in the cloudy cells (median zone). This phenomenon is called *interference.*

The exact inheritance patterns of the various avian pigments are not fully known; however, when they are altered, leading to an abnormal plumage pigmentation (mutation), the operative mechanisms can be quite reasonably supposed.

The phenomenon that occurs most in *Agapornis* is schizochroism. The coloration abnormalities are due to the absence or the presence of the above mentioned pigments, together or not, and in different proportions. We have the following phenomena:

• Melanism—either the overproduction of melanin or an abnormal localization of the melanin (in areas not normally dark).

• Dilution—the partial or total decrease of the pigments normally present. This process is not totally understood.

• Leucism—the plumage coloration becomes partially or totally white; the eyes remain black.

• Albinism—the total absence of plumage pigments, with red eyes (no pigments). Partial albinism also occurs.

• Schizochroism—there are three kinds known: (1) Fawn—the total or partial loss of eumelanin. The remaining phaeomelanin gives a brownish coloration to the plumage. The eyes are light brown or reddish. (2) Gray—the total or partial loss of phaeomelanin, which gives a grayish tone to the plumage. (3) Lutino—the total or

Gray Green *roseicollis*. This is probably the first example of gray schizochroism in *Agapornis*. The Gray factor produces a gray shade over all the body, giving a slightly dark phenotype and a grayish blue rump.

West German Fallow *roseicollis*. Here you see an example of true fawn schizochroism.

partial loss of both melanins (eumelanin and phaeomelanin). The resulting carotenoid predominance gives a yellow coloration to the bird. The eyes are red.

Additionally, some colorations are due to structural changes in the feathers. Three structural patterns may be distinguished:

• Blue—occurs when there is total or partial absence of carotenoids (psittacins). The blue color is produced by light dispersion in the median zone (cloudy cells) over or through the remaining melanin pigments. This is a light-interference phenomenon.

• Violet—occurs due to an increased diameter of the medullar zone of the feather and the enlargement of the feather's cortex and barbs. As a result, the long light waves are absorbed, darkening the plumage with a violet color tone since the shorter waves are reflected; i.e., light rays close to the violet spectrum (420-380 nm).

• Dark—occurs due to the narrowing of the feather's median zone (cloudy cells), producing extensive light absorption, darkening the entire plumage.

While the phenomena described above occur widely in avian species, the colorations described above are more commonly identified with psittacines.

A better understanding of these phenomena may be obtained by the examining the schematized transverse sections of *Agapornis* feathers.

Lutino *roseicollis*. The white rump and primaries together with red eyes characterize the Ino factor.

NOMENCLATURE USED IN *AGAPORNIS* MUTATIONS.

It is necessary here to provide a brief overview of the terms used to denominate lovebird mutations and their combinations. All the

SCHEMATIC FEATHER CUTS WITH PIGMENT DISTRIBUTIONS OF THE MAIN AGAPORNIS MUTATIONS AND FORMS.

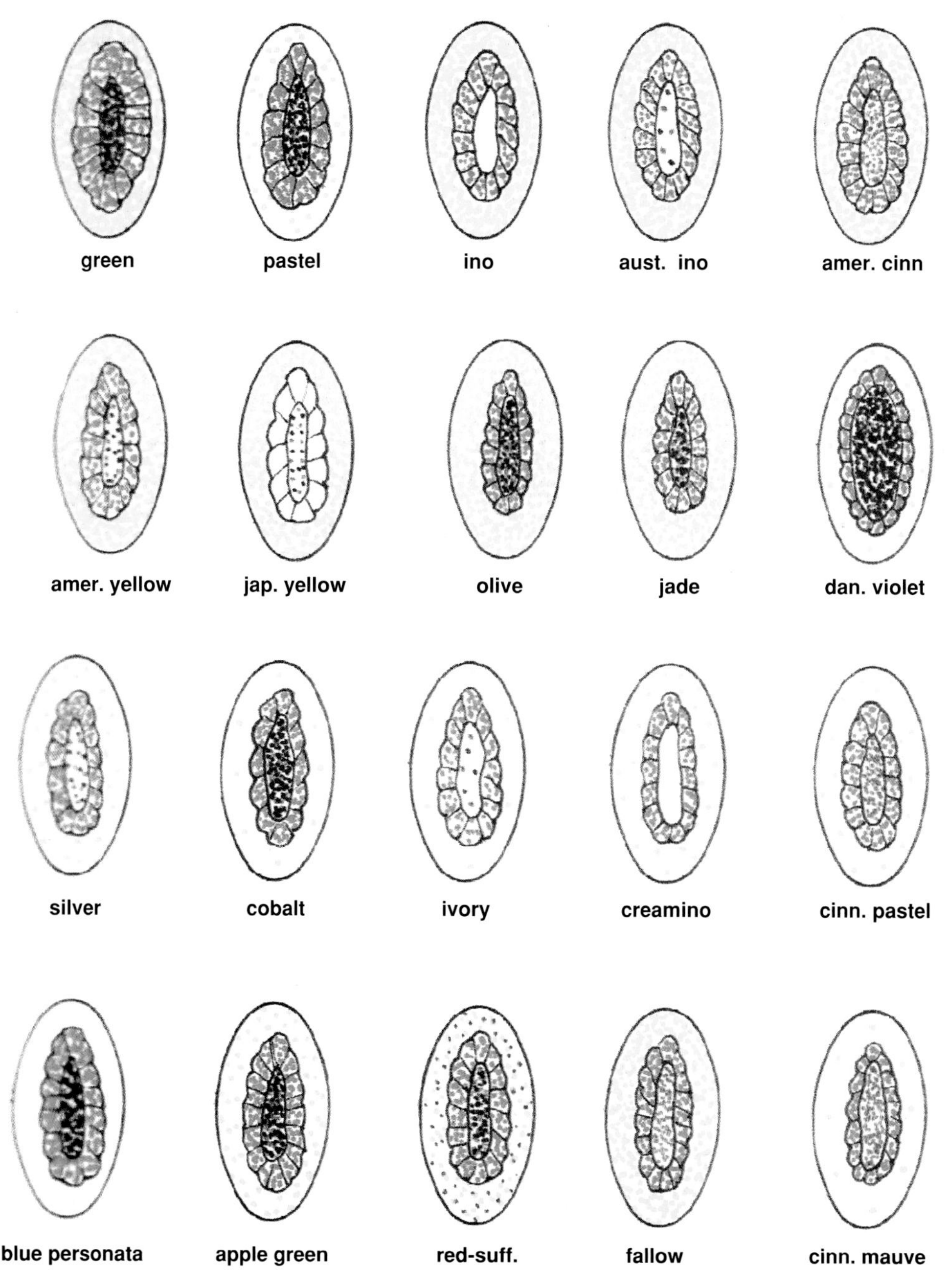

mutations result in colorations that differ from the wild-colored phenotypes, which are often referred to as Normal, or Green (as this happens to be the case with all *Agapornis* forms).

Combinations of the mutations accumulate the names of the mutations they originated from. Thus, if we combine the American Cinnamon and the American Yellow factors, and the resultant bird is homozygous for both, its phenotype will be designated with the names of the two source mutations: Cinnamon American Yellow. So we can get Cinnamon Slate, Olive (Dark Green) American Yellow, Whiteface Cinnamon, Orangeface Lutino, etc.

Danish Violet Cobalt.

However, some combinations exhibit very distinctive color tones and have been given separate names. For example:

- Mustard, which is Australian Ino (Cinnamon) Dark Green (Olive).
- Ivory, which is "Blue" Australian Ino (Cinnamon).
- Creamino, which is "Blue" Lutino, also erroneously called Albino.
- Olive, which is Dark Green, i.e, double Dark-factored Green.
- Mauve: Dark Pastel, Slate, i.e., double Dark-factored Pastel.

The last two illustrate the peculiar terms employed for combinations involving the Dark pattern, or Dark factor. In Green birds (yellow): one Dark factor = Medium Green, or Jade. Two Dark factors = Dark Green, or Olive. In non-Green birds (not yellow): one Dark factor = Medium Pastel, or Cobalt. Two Dark factors = Dark Pastel, or Slate, or Mauve.

GENETICS: AN APPROACH

Matters involving genetics are misunderstood most of the time. In general, breeders and aviculturists have a prejudice against this science. The mere mention of this word is enough to put them in a defensive position: "Genetics? Too complicated, I don't think about it. It's for scientists, not for me!"

Well, indeed you are a scientist! That's right! Bird breeding is a science, and we must always be increasing our know-how, no matter how experienced we are. You will see that a basic understanding of genetics can lead to enormous success in your *Agapornis* breeding.

Let's go, my dear scientist friend, don't run away yet; we are just about to enter the marvelous world of genetics and agapornism.

Dark Apple Green *roseicollis.* Note the brownish green shade suffused on the gray color; this is due to a partial dilution produced by the Whiteface factor.

WHAT IS GENETICS?

Genetics is a word that comes from Latin and means "birth", or "generation." Genetics is a science that studies the birth, the genesis of life, and associated laws and phenomena.

The *gene* is the fundamental entity in genetics. It is a particular nucleic-acid molecule structure that is responsible for building every one of a living being's structures. It resembles a computer program specifically designed to do a certain kind of work. Sometimes more than one gene contributes to a result, interacting with others; this is true of practically all mutant genes involved in the plumage color of lovebirds.

An organism's genes are not a random collection; instead, they are organized into numerous filament-like structures, the chromosomes, along which they occupy well-defined places called *loci.* Each *locus* (the singular form of loci) is the section occupied by one gene responsible for a certain character.

Dark Green Australian Ino (Mustard) *roseicollis*. Here double Dark factors are combined with the Australian Ino (Cinnamon) factor.

Conventionally, genes are represented by alphabetic characters (*A, X, Y, Z,* etc.). For example: let's use the letter *y* to refer to the gene which is responsible for the "Blue" in *roseicollis*. Whenever we mention the *y*, we are referring to the "Blue," or Pastel, factor. To avoid confusion and misunderstandings, we should never use the same alphabetic character to designate different genes.

As an appendix to this book, I have prepared a list of the factors found in *Agapornis* genetics. The reader may find it helpful to consult this list as we proceed through the following examples.

Let's suppose that *y* is on a certain *roseicollis* chromosome. Now, the chromosomes are structures that can be compared to filaments or chains, linking thousands of genes. The number of chromosomes is constant in each animal or vegetable species. The chromosomes occur in pairs which are designated by numbers. The two chromosomes of the pair are *homologous* to one another, and their genes are known, locus to locus, as *alleles.*

The usefulness of having paired chromosomes and genes is

Australian Ino (Cinnamon) *roseicollis.* An example of partial lutinism in *Agapornis*. This factor is allele of the American Ino.

Dark Green American Cinnamon (American Mustard or American Cinnamon Olive) *roseicollis*.

obvious when we have to form a new living being. The *egg* is formed by the union of two cells: the ovum and the spermatozoan, that are the female and male reproductive cells, respectively. It happens that each of the parents supplies a certain "half" of their genetic pattern. In the creation of a new living being it is necessary that chromosomes are paired one to one, gene to gene (locus to locus), forming homologous chromosomes, thus making possible the exchange of "genetical cargo" between the two parents.

We will obtain a new individual, formed by half of the father's genes and half of the mother's genes. Occasionally, some of these genes suffer alterations, which most of the time are a genetic "error." These lead the genes to manifest their characters in different ways, breaking the usual tendency of individuals to remain similar to their own species. Such variations are called *mutations* if can they be inherited and *modifications* or *fluctuations* if not.

Mutations are the result of spontaneous natural phenomena, but they can also be induced in the laboratory with unforseeable results. We can observe two kinds of mutations: (1) genetic mutations that are inherited and (2) somatic mutations that occur when the cells are modified during their embryonic evolution; this can occur in just an area or body region. The genotype can be completely normal, and there is no transmission of the affected characters to a descendant. Somatic mutations can occasionally be observed in lovebirds; the half-siders are a good example.

Let's consider in more detail how a true mutation might have appeared: There is at least one pair of genes in *Agapornis personata* that is responsible for the presence of a substance called melanin. Eventually an "error" occurred in one of these genes, rendering it incapable of producing melanin. Melanin production was reduced, but it continued to be produced under the control of the normal allele, so no visible alterations could be detected. Eventually, two of these faulty genes came together in the same bird. There was no possibility of producing any melanin, and a totally nonmelanic bird was born: a Lutino *personata*. The faulty gene could be inherited in the normal fashion by a descendant, so a true mutation appeared.

This time there was a change in plumage color, but it might have been in eye color or in the shape of the bones or the beak, etc. Genetic "errors" do not always produce visible results, and sometimes they are fatal. Imperceptible or nonviable mutations can also occur.

A good understanding of the above-mentioned example will enable you to understand everything to come. The concepts of dominant and recessive, chromosomal mutation, and an idea on somatic mutation were presented in the example above; let's review it more fully:

Australian White (Primrose) *roseicollis*. The greenish blue suffusion on the back is characteristic of the Australian Yellow factor.

Pied Danish Violet Cobalt (Pied Violet Medium Pastel) *roseicollis*.

DOMINANCE

A *dominant* gene is one which expresses the character even though its paired allele is different (i.e., the organism is heterozygous). In the cited example we've seen that just one normal (dominant) gene is enough to produce melanin at levels that

Apple Green Australian Ino (Apple Green Ivory) *roseicollis.* This combination consists of one Whiteface, one Pastel, and two Australian Ino factors. (Male).

produce a normal phenotype. Dominant genes are represented by capital letters. We will call *I* the normal gene that produces melanin in *personata.* Its alternative is indicated by *i,* which will provide the Lutino phenotype when present on both chromosomes (homozygosity).

Thus a gene that expresses its character only when homozygous, such as the *i* (Ino factor) in the above cited example, is called *recessive.* Put another way, *I* means the presence of melanin, while *i* results in the absence of melanin.

We can have three possible combinations: *II,* normal; *Ii,* heterozygote for no melanin (or, split for Lutino); *ii* Lutino, homozygote for no melanin. We can understand that the cited mutation occurred due to the loss of something that produced melanin, and so it was called the Ino factor; in *personata* this gene is a recessive autosomal (not linked to sex). The great majority of mutant genes are recessives!

INCOMPLETE DOMINANCE

Incomplete dominance, or codominance, is a genetic inheritance pattern where the genes are neither dominant nor

American White *roseicollis,* a combination Pastel and American Yellow.

recessive. These genes, when heterozygous, produce a phenotype intermediate between the homozygous and the nonmutant.

There is a gene in *roseicollis* which is responsible for decreasing the cloudy cells and increasing the feather's medulla. When it is heterozygous (single factor) it will modify the phenotype, darkening the color and tingeing the feathers with a violet cast, most visible in the rump, which will become a strong bluish violet. This same gene when homozygous will produce a darker bird with a deep violet

Whiteface American White. The Whiteface factor adds a dilution that interacts with the American Yellow factor, giving a marbled yellow pattern in the back and mantle.

Apple Green Lutino *roseicollis*.

color tone all over the body. We are talking about the Danish Violet factor. The alteration produced by a single gene is enough to produce a different phenotype, and when homozygous it will generate yet a third, different phenotype.

The Danish Violet is a codominant, or incomplete dominant, mutation and can be symbolized like so:

vv, not Violet; *Vv*, single-factor Violet; *VV*, double-factor Violet.

The incompletely dominant genes in *Agapornis* are expressed in a quantitative way the great majority of the time; this way, some of them can also be included as cumulative, or

Apple Green American White *roseicollis*. This bird is molting.

quantitative, inheritance. This terminology is more correct when there are two or more pairs of genes involved in the same character (a polygenic character).

So, we must always specify to which gene any other is dominant or recessive—and these terms cannot be used among genes in different loci. Inheritance among genes in different loci is always interactive.

DOMINANCE'S VARIABILITY

Depending on the complex of genetic factors, genes can manifest their characters differently. The capacity of expression for a given character and its variations among those individuals showing it is called the *expressivity of a gene.* This means that a gene can express its character differently in different situations, as we can see in the American Pied factor in *roseicollis*, which varies enormously in its expressivity: there are birds ranging from a very lightly pied to a heavily pied phenotype.

Dilute Green *personata* split for Ino. Here the single Ino factor lightens the overall color.

The occurrence of gene interactions confuses genetic analyses, as we can see with the autosomal recessive Ino factor in *personata*. It interacts with the Dilute factor *d*, generating a bright yellow phenotype with black eyes: *ddIi*, Dilute Green *personata* heterozygous (split) for Ino namely, the Yellow *personata*. This phenotype allows the Ino factor to be easily identified, and that's quite important in aviculture. Non-Dilute split-for-Ino birds are hardly identified with certainty.

Dark Green (Olive) *personata*. A juvenile bird.

Dilute Blue *personata* split for Ino. The Ino, when present with a double Dilute factor, will lighten the colors. This allows a split bird to be easily identified by the snow white color on the back.

A gene that always expresses its character is said to have an optimum expressivity. The Red-suffusion factor is an example of a low-expressivity gene. Gene expressivity can be analyzed and measured in terms of genic *penetration*, which is nothing more than the proportion in a population of individuals that have the same genotype and show a certain character.

GENETIC BASIS APPLIED TO AGAPORNISM

The genetic basis for treating simple single-gene effects were first described by a monk named Gregor Johann Mendel, born in 1822 in Silesia. Mendel, in his work entitled *Experiments with Plant Hybridization*, showed us the main rules of inheritance. Even today, after we discovered that several other mechanisms are involved, the "Mendelian laws" are still taught worldwide in schools.

MENDEL'S FIRST LAW

We have already seen the concepts of dominance and recessiveness, which are essential to a good understanding of Mendelism. First, we will work with "pure" bloodlines. *A bloodline is the group of direct descendants from a common ancestor.*

Nowadays, lovebirds of a pure bloodline are difficult to find, due to the extent of previous matings. This does not mean we have hybrids, or *mestizos*. We just have carriers of several pairs of mutant genes; i.e., heterozygotes, or splits, for several mutations. The term *split* is commonly used in aviculture as a synonym for *heterozygote*.

We must understand that *a pure line is one that carries just one pair of mutant genes.* So first we will work just with pure lines: blues will transmit just blue, the yellows just yellow and so on. The generations of descendants are designated as F1 (first generation), F2 (second generation), F3 (third generation), etc.

For our first examples, we shall consider factors found in *A. roseicollis*.

Example 1: Green (YY) x Pastel (yy).

	Y	Y
y	Yy	Yy
y	Yy	Yy

100% Green /Pastel (Yy, Green split, or heterozygous, for Pastel).

Each of the parents contribute one of their genes, producing the descendants *Yy*: Greens split for Pastel.

IMPORTANT: The green color is produced by a schizochroic interaction of several genes. The gene *Y* is not by itself responsible for the green color but is only one of the contributing factors. Here, *Y* represents the absence of the Pastel factor.

Example 2: Green /Pastel (Yy) x Green /Pastel (Yy).

	Y	y
Y	YY	Yy
y	Yy	yy

0.5Y x 0.5Y = 0.25: 25% Green (homozygote, YY).

2(0.5Y x 0.5y) = 2(0.25): 50% Green /Pastel (heterozygote for Pastel, Yy).

0.5y x 0.5y = 0.25: 25% Pastel (homozygote, yy).

Phenotypes: 75% Green, 25% Pastel.

We can observe a proportion 3:1 (Green:Pastel), due to the sharing of the heterozygote gene pair *Yy*. This segregation is regular when related to pure lines because of the chromosomal division.

This is Mendel's first law, also known as the law of segregation, or pureness, of the gametes. It can be stated like this: *When segregation of a pair of genes occurs, the gametes are transmitted to their descendants in a frequency of 50%.* A different pairing, Green /Pastel x Pastel, provides a further illustration of the first law.

Example 3: Green /Pastel (Yy) x Pastel (yy).

	Y	y
y	Yy	yy
y	Yy	yy

2(0.5Y x 0.5y) = 2(0.25): 50% Green /Pastel (Yy).

2(0.5y x 0.5y) = 2(0.25): 50% Pastel (yy).

MENDEL'S SECOND LAW

Application of the first Mendelian law to *Agapornis* breeding is very restricted, as the interactions between genes were not considered at the time of its elaboration. The schizochroic nature of *Agapornis* coloration is such that all characters are the result of genic interaction. Therefore, the second Mendelian law, which considers two or more allele pairs at the same time, is more pertinent.

The allelic segregation in this case occurs independently for each pair of genes: each parent will produce gametes that carry just one allele of each pair of genes, as the first law states. To illustrate this, let us consider the American Yellow and the Pastel factors. Note: genes *A* and *Y* respectively signify the absence of American Yellow (*a*) and Pastel (*y*).

American Yellow (*aaYY*) x Pastel (*AAyy*) yields 100% Green /Amer.-Yellow /Pastel (*AaYy*).

The double heterozygote *AaYy* is phenotypically green, as both of the genes involved are recessives and are heterozygous. We have a bird that exhibits non-Yellow (A) and non-Pastel (Y). It is a bird that does not show any mutant characteristics; instead, it has the green color of the "wild," non-mutant phenotype. Pairing these among themselves:

Example 4: Green /Amer.-Yellow /Pastel (AaYy) x Green / Amer.-Yellow /Pastel (AaYy).

	AY	Ay	aY	ay
AY	AAYY	AAYy	AaYY	AaYy
Ay	AAYy	AAyy	AaYy	Aayy
aY	AaYY	AaYy	aaYY	aaYy
ay	AaYy	Aayy	aaYy	aayy

Each square corresponds to a frequency rate of 1/16 (6.25%).

6.25% Green (AAYY).

12.5% Green /Pastel (AAYy).

12.5% Green /Amer.-Yellow (AaYY).

25.0% Green /Amer.-Yellow / Pastel (AaYy).

6.25% Pastel (AAyy).

12.5% Pastel /Amer.-Yellow (Aayy).

12.5% Amer. Yellow /Pastel (aaYy).

6.25% Amer. Yellow (aaYY).
6.25% Silver (Pastel Amer. Yellow, aayy).

Note that the interaction between the genes *y* and *a* produce a third phenotype, the Silver, or Pastel American Yellow, also known as White.

The above example yields four phenotypes: Green; American Yellow (American Golden Cherry); Pastel; and Pastel American Yellow, respectively in the following proportion: 9:3:3:1. This is a consequence of Mendel's second law (the independent segregation of alleles—it is important to add that combinations that do not follow the Mendelian law also exist).

Example 4 is typical of the great majority of the *Agapornis* inheritance patterns and exhibits the following phenomena: dominance, recessiveness, and gene interaction (Pastel interacts with American Yellow to produce an additional color).

We can still verify that: the homozygotes for two pairs of genes appear at a rate of 1/16 (6.25%); heterozygotes for one pair of genes at 2/16 (12.50%); and heterozygotes for two pairs of genes appear at 4/16 (25%).

Example 5: Pastel /Amer.-Yellow (Aayy) x Pastel /Amer.-Yellow (Aayy).

	Ay	ay
Ay	AAyy	Aayy
ay	Aayy	aayy

25% Pastel (AAyy); 50% Pastel / Amer.-Yellow (Aayy); 25% Silver (Pastel Amer. Yellow, aayy).

In the above example, two allele pairs are involved, with both parents homozygous for Pastel (*y*). The rate obtained follows Mendel's first law since there is no variability at the Pastel factor's locus.

For another example, let us combine the Dilute and the Blue mutations of *Agapornis personata.*

Example 6: Blue (aaDD) x Dilute (AAdd) yields 100% Green / Blue /Dilute (AaDd).

Pairing Green /Blue /Dilute (AaDd) x Green /Blue /Dilute (AaDd):

	AD	Ad	aD	ad
AD	AADD	AADd	AaDD	AaDd
Ad	AADd	AAdd	AaDd	Aadd
aD	AaDD	AaDd	aaDD	aaDd
ad	AaDd	Aadd	aaDd	aadd

6.25% Green (AADD).
12.5% Green /Dilute (AADd).
12.5% Dilute /Blue (Aadd).
25.0% Green /Blue /Dilute (AaDd).
12.5% Green /Blue (AaDD).
6.25% Dilute (AAdd).
12.5% Blue /Dilute (aaDd).
6.25% Blue (aaDD).
6.25% Dilute Blue (aadd).

We could analyze three pairs of genes at the same time. In Example 7, continuing with personata, we will pair the Dilute Blue with a Lutino (represented as a; non-Lutino is A).

Dilute Blue (IIaadd) x Lutino (iiAADD) yields 100% Green / Dilute /Blue /Lutino (IiAaDd).

These offspring are now paired: IiAaDd x IiAaDd.

	IAD	IAd	IaD	Iad	iAD	iAd	iaD	iad
IAD	IIAADD	IIAADd	IIAaDD	IIAaDd	IiAADD	IiAADd	IiAaDD	IiAaDd
IAd	IIAADd	IIAAdd	IIAaDd	IIAadd	IiAADd	IiAAdd	IiAaDd	IiAadd
IaD	IIAaDD	IIAaDd	IIaaDD	IIaaDd	IiAaDD	IiAaDd	IiaaDD	IiaaDd
Iad	IIAaDd	IIAadd	IIaaDd	IIaadd	IiAaDd	IiAadd	IiaaDd	Iiaadd
iAD	IiAADD	IiAADd	IiAaDD	IiAaDd	iiAADD	iiAADd	iiAaDD	iiAaDd
iAd	IiAADd	IiAAdd	IiAaDd	IiAadd	iiAADd	iiAAdd	iiAaDd	iiAadd
iaD	IiAaDD	IiAaDd	IiaaDD	IiaaDd	iiAaDD	iiAaDd	iiaaDD	iiaaDd
iad	IiAaDd	IiAadd	IiaaDd	Iiaadd	iiAaDd	iiAadd	iiaaDd	iiaadd

From this pairing we obtain 27 genotypes. The interaction between the factors in question here is such that the resulting eight visually different phenotypes are not those we might expect theoretically (the hyphen means that having either allele present will not affect the phenotype): See box below.

Now, Mendel's second law, which we have just seen, does not apply in all cases; it refers only to genes that occur on nonhomologous chromosomes; that is, to genes that are not *linked.*

LINKAGE AND CROSSING OVER

On the same chromosome the genes are linked and tend to keep together, a phenomenon called *linkage.* Indeed, a chromosome consists of a chain of genes. The genes are lined up, and, when they are duplicated, identical genes should result. However, the practical results show us that gene recombination can nevertheless occur, as a result of another phenomenon: *crossing over.*

Crossing over is an occasional exchange, without

We have the following eight different phenotypes

phenotype	**genotype**	**frequency:**		
green	I_A_D	27/64	=	42,20%
yellow (dilute green)	IIA_dd	3/64	=	4.68%
yellow/ino	IiAdd	6/64	=	9,38%
blue	I_aaD_	9/64	=	14,06%
dilute blue	IIaadd	1/64	=	1,57%
dilute blue/ino	Iiaadd	2/64	=	3,13%
lutino	iiA_	12/64	=	18,75%
albino	iiaa_	4/64	=	6,25%

The _ means that any gene which is present will not modify the phenotype.

preset rules and at no particular point, of parts of the filaments (chromatids) of homologous chromosomes, in a tetrad (the group of four chromatids formed in the course of duplication of the homologous chromosomes). After an initial intertwining, the filaments repel one another, allowing an exchange of fragments bearing several genes. This mechanism accounts for just one aspect of the impossibility of recombination predicted by Mendel's second law.

The crossing-over rate between two genes is directly proportional to the distance along the chromosome between them: the farther apart, the greater the crossing rate, up to a maximum of 50%.

In *Agapornis*, the linkage phenomenon, together with crossing over, occurs clearly in *roseicollis*: Let's consider the Dark factor (*E*) and the Pastel factor (*y*). When there is a complete linkage between them, each gamete shall carry either *EY* or *ey* and there will be no recombination. In this case there will be just two kinds of gametes: *EY* (50%) and *ey* (50%). However, we know that Dark Pastels (Mauves, or Slates) do occur; this is genetically *Ey*, indicating that

Example 8: Dark Green (Olive, EEYY) x Pastel (eeyy) yields 100% Medium Green (Jade, EeYy). These are next paired among themselves: EeYy x EeYy:

	EY	Ey	eY	ey
EY	EEYY	EEYy	EeYY	EeYy
Ey	EEYy	EEyy	EeYy	Eeyy
eY	EeYY	EeYy	eeYY	eeYy
ey	EeYy	Eeyy	eeYy	eeyy

crossing over occurred.

Theoretically, we expect Dark Pastels (*EEyy*) at a rate of 1/16, or 6.25%. We've observed that their real frequency is 1/93, or 1.07%. A crossing rate of 1.07% means that approximately 1.10% were crossed over. So we have *Ey* = 0.55% and *eY* = 0.55%, yielding a sum of 1.10%. Thus 98.90% experienced no crossing over.

Let's see it graphically to have a better understanding:

(Facing page)

The close linkage between these genes doesn't favor crossing-over, as shown by the reduction of the expected rate of 6.25% to an actual rate of 1.07% for the Dark Pastel.

We distinguish two kinds of heterozygotes for Dark-and-Pastel-factored birds: Type I is *EYey*, and Type II is *EyeY*. Both birds above are Medium Green, yet only the Type II will produce Dark Pastels (*EEyy*) at the Mendelian rate. We mainly need to get Medium Greens Type II by pairing Medium Greens Type I to Dark Pastels at a higher rate.

The highest crossing rate is 50%, which signifies an exchange of 100% of genes between two cells.

"Crossing-over," graphical example:

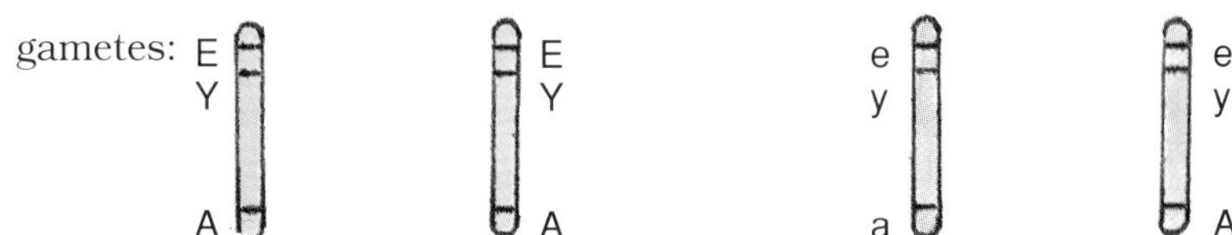

A) crossing occurrence between distant genes

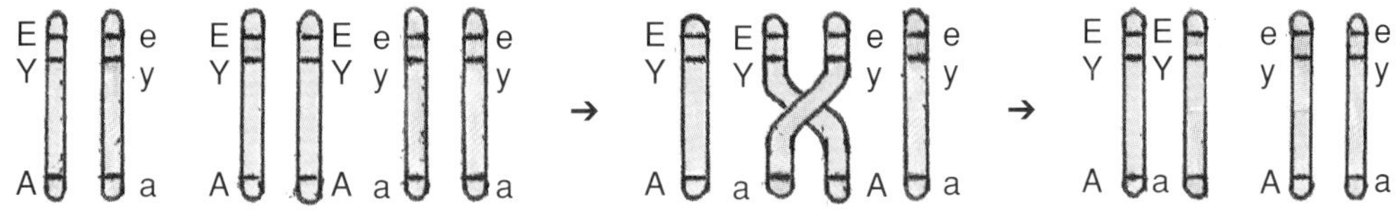

b) very close genes won't suffer crossing-over:

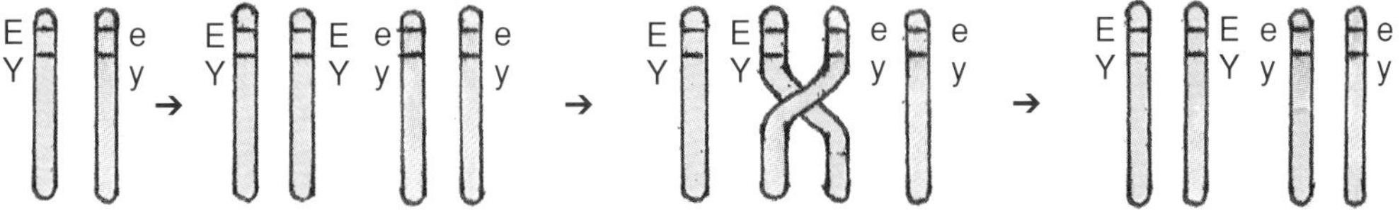

SEX-LINKED GENES

There are several genes that do not manifest their characters in the usual fashion, and in some matings we can notice that certain phenotypes appear predominantly in females, rather than in males.

The occurrence of genes that are linked to sex is known as *sex-linkage*. These genes are located on the sex chromosomes (heterosomes), generally in birds designated by the letters Z and W. The use of Z and W means automatically that the heterogametic sex is the female: the males are ZZ, and the females are ZW. The chromosomes Z and W are analogues of X and Y, respectively, of the other animal classes (mammals, some insects, etc.).

The use of XY and XX with birds is completely wrong, because once it is applied, it is assumed that the heterogametic sex is represented by the males, which isn't the case with birds.

A sex-linked gene, if recessive, will express its character in birds only when homozygotic (present on both Zs); in the females, which are hemizygotic, we'll get the phenotype in question with just one factor. This way, the recessive sex-linked characters will appear more frequently in females, increasing the mutant female population in relation to the male population. This fact is easily observed in the Cinnamon and Ino factors in *roseicollis*. Let's first examine the Ino factor.

Example 9: American Lutino male (ZiZiYY) x Pastel female (ZIWyy).

	ZiY	ZiY
ZIy	ZIZiYy	ZIZiYy
Wy	ZiWYy	ZiWYy

50% Green /Ino /Pastel males (ZIZiYy); 50% Lutino /Pastel females (ZiWYy).

Example 10: Green /Ino /Pastel male (ZIZiYy) x Pastel female (ZIWyy):

	ZIY	ZIy	ZiY	Ziy
ZIy	ZIZIYy	ZIZIyy	ZIZiYy	ZIZiyy
Wy	ZIWYy	ZIWyy	ZiWYy	ZiWyy

Males: 12.5% Green /Pastel (ZIZIYy); 12.5% Green /Ino / Pastel (ZIZiYy); 12.5 % Pastel (ZIZIyy); 12.5% Pastel /Ino (ZIZiyy).

Females: 12.5% Green /Pastel (ZIWYy); 12.5% Pastel (ZIWyy); 12.5% Lutino /Pastel (ZiWYy); 12.5% Creamino (ZiWyy).

Note: the Ino and Pastel factors combined one with another will produce a different phenotype that was absent so far: the Creamino, or Pastel Ino.

Let's look at another example of a roseicollis sex-linked factor, American Cinnamon.

Example 11: American Pied Green male (ZCZCPP) x American Cinnamon Green female (ZcWpp).

	ZCP	ZCP
Zcp	ZCZcPp	ZCZcPp
Wp	ZCWPp	ZCWPp

50% Pied Green /Cinnamon males (ZCZcPp); 50% Pied Green females (ZCWPp).

(Here Mendelian inheritance is adopted for the Pied factor, even though there are additional genetic phenomena involved.)

Example12: Pied Green / Cinnamon male (ZCZcPp) x American Cinnamon female (ZcWpp).

	ZCP	ZCp	ZcP	Zcp
Zcp	ZCZcPp	ZCZcpp	ZcZcPp	ZcZcpp
Wp	ZCWPp	ZCWpp	ZcWPp	ZcWpp

Males: 12.5% Pied Green /Cinn. (ZCZcPp); 12.5% Green /Cinn. (ZCZcpp); 12.5% Pied Green Cinn. (ZcZcPp); 12.5% Cinnamon (ZcZcpp).

Females: 12.5% Pied Green (ZCWPp); 12.5% Green (ZCWpp); 12.5% Pied Cinnamon (ZcWPp); 12.5% Cinnamon (ZcWpp).

Example 13: Australian Lutino male (ZiaZia) x American Lutino female (ZiW).

	Zia	Zia
Zi	ZiaZi	ZiaZi
W	ZiaW	ZiaW

50% Australian Lutino /Amer. Ino males (ZiaZi); 50% Australian Lutino females (ZiaW).

Example 14: Australian Lutino/ Amer. Ino male (ZiaZi) x Green female (ZIW).

	Zia	Zi
ZI	ZIZia	ZIZi
W	ZiaW	ZiW

Males: 25% Green /Austr. Ino (ZIZia); 25% Green /Amer. Ino (ZIZi).

Females: 25% Australian Lutino (ZiaW); 25% American Lutino (ZiW).

MULTIPLE ALLELES

Some instances of polyallelia, or multiple alleles, are found in the genus *Agapornis*. In this phenomenon, there is more than one allele for the same locus and character. This is the result of different mutations that occurred in the same gene on different occasions.

The Ino factor in *roseicollis* is a good example of multiple alleles: two seperate mutations occurred separately in two distant places in the world: one in Australia in 1957 and the other in the USA in 1973. The Australian mutation, erroneously known as Australian Cinnamon, is in truth a schizochroic partial lutinism, while its American allele is a classic schizochroic lutinism. Both genes are at the same locus. The Australian allele is dominant to the American. If analyzed separately, both are recessives to the normal gene.

EPISTASIS

Epistasis is a genetic phenomenon that occurs when a certain character dominates over another nonallelic gene.

One good example involves the American Ino factor and the Dark factor, which are found on different chromosomes. When they occur together in the same individual, the Lutino trait dominates. We cannot detect the Dark factor, although the bird in question is genetically a Dark Lutino or Lutino Olive.

We can say that the Ino factor is epistatic to the Dark factor, or that the Dark is hypostatic to the Ino. It is important to note that only the Ino factor's American allele is epistatic to the Dark factor. The Ino factor's Australian allele interacts with Dark factor to produce a mustard-colored phenotype (see Mustards).

Another example may be found in *personata*, where the Ino factor is epistatic to the *personata* Dilute factor.

Epistasis is a phenomenon in which a trait manifests itself over another produced by a nonallelic gene. The epistatic gene itself may be either dominant or recessive.

LETHAL GENES

Though lethal genes are not generally uncommon, in *Agapornis* none have been identified scientifically. Such genes may be sex-linked or autosomal. They become manifest when progeny or a certain genotype or phenotype don't appear, or when the young die.

Several aviculturists have suggested that the Ino factors in both *roseicollis* (sex-linked) and *personata* (autosomal) sometimes occur in a lethal pattern, mainly in matings involving two Ino parents. This crossing usually produces chicks that die when they are a few days old.

Our experience suggests that this situation is a recessive pleiotropism (an additional, seemingly unrelated effect of a gene) of the Ino factors. The young birds seem to be immunodeficient; perhaps in these Inos the immune system matures more slowly than in other *Agapornis* mutations.

There is a critical period between the first and the sixteenth days of life during which the chicks are extremely susceptible to diseases. The parents must be kept healthy and even sometimes under antibiotic therapy, together with the young; this will produce a decline in mortality that will tend to zero. This observation brings to us the following postulate: *Behavioral problems excepted, when chicks in the nest die prematurely, it is an important sign that one or both parents carry some disease, visible or not!*

A bird's rump is an important area for identifying carried factors. On the left is a normal *roseicollis*. Right below, a Medium Green (one Dark factor). Right above, a Violet Green (one Danish Violet factor).

Nyasa Lovebird. Pure birds do show a bright red orange front contrasting with a deep green. A slightly yellowish band in the nape is observed.

***Agapornis roseicollis* and its mutations**

PEACH-FACE MUTATIONS

Agapornis roseicollis, the Peach-face Lovebird is the most popular species in the genus. Its wild phenotype is mainly green, with forehead red, throat and upper breast rose pink, iris brown, and rump bright blue. So far, the Peach-face Lovebirds have produced the largest number of mutations in the genus. There are twenty mutant genes, which can form thousands of genotypical and not many fewer phenotypical combinations. (See facing page).

Violet pastel *roseicollis* (One Danish Violet factor). Even without a Dark factor the Danish violet effect is considerably stronger than the comparable American Violet.

THE PASTEL FACTOR

Synonyms: Pastel Blue, Dutch Blue.

The Pastel factor appeared in 1963 in Holland in Mr. Habets's aviaries. It is the most common *roseicollis* mutation and probably the commonest phenotype among all *agapornis*; it can be said there are more Pastels than normal Greens.

We purposely didn't use the terms *Blue* or *Pastel Blue* here. This is because this factor is nothing but a psittacin diluter, which causes a partial absence of the carotenoids. When heterozygous, the effect is almost imperceptible: split birds are barely lighter than non-splits. This gene when homozygous leads to a large, but not total, psittacin dilution, producing a foggy bluish bird. So, *this is not a truly blue bird but a dilute green, in which the visible coloration is a foggy blue.* So we have the name *Pastel.*

PEACH-FACE LOVEBIRD, *A. ROSEICOLLIS*

Factor	*Normal Allele*	*Mutant Allele*	*Mode of Inheritance*
Pastel (Blue)	*Y*	*y*	AR
American Pied	*p*	*P*	AD
Dark	*e(1, 2, 3)*	*E(1, 2, 3)*	AC
American Yellow	*A*	*a*	AR
Graywing	*A*	*a2*	AR
Japanese Yellow	*J*	*j*	AR
American Ino	Z^I	Z^i	SLR
Australian Ino	Z^I	Z^{ia}	SLR
American Cinnamon	Z^C	Z^c	SLR
West German Fallow	*F*	*f*	AR
East German Fallow	*F2*	*f2*	AR
Danish Violet	*v*	*V*	AC
American Violet	*v2*	*V2*	AC
Australian Yellow	*Pr*	*pr*	AR
Whiteface	*W*	*w*	AR
Orangeface	*l*	*L*	AC
Red-suffusion	*S*	*s*	AR
Red-eye	*r*	*R*	AD
Gray	*G*	*g*	AR
Gray Pastel	*gp*	*Gp*	AD

MUTATIONS IN THE GENUS *AGAPORNIS*

The factors found in lovebirds are listed by species. The symbols for both the normal and the mutant alleles are followed by an abbreviation indicating the mode of inheritance, as follows: AR: autosomal recessive; AC: autosomal codominant or incompletely dominant; SLR: sex-linked recessive; AD: autosomal dominant.

In the case of some mutations, the mode of inheritance shown here is only a conjecture, awaiting further research; these factors are marked with an asterisk (*).

Danish Violet Cobalt (Danish Violet Medium Pastel) *roseicollis*. This bird has just one Violet factor (heterozygous for Violet).

The true Blue would be characterized by a total lack of psittacin; so far there is no such *roseicollis* variety, probably due to genic interaction. *No truly blue mutation has occurred in the Peach-face Lovebird.*

We consider it very proper to refer to this psittacin-diluting gene as the Pastel factor. Its combinations shall receive the name of the other factor combined with the term *Pastel*: e.g., Pastel American Cinnamon; Violet Pastel; etc. Some combinations have particular names as a result of widespread use and a very distinct phenotype: Creamino (Pastel Ino); Ivory (Pastel Australian Ino, or Pastel Australian Cinnamon); etc.

The Pastel factor's mode of inheritance is autosomal recessive, and its alleles are symbolized by *y* and *Y*, the latter denoting its absence. That means that whenever it is heterozygous, it won't manifest its character, except in the instance of the double heterozygote for Pastel and Whiteface popularly known as Apple Green.

The color tones found among Pastel birds are extremely variable. The color even changes according to the angle of incidence of the light reflected from the feathers. Males are generally more greenish, so possibly this phenomenon is influenced by the sex chromosomes. Also, like the psittacins, the melanins are arranged in the feather structures into prisms that refract light. As different amounts of light are reflected, we will perceive different color tones.

Creamino (Pastel Ino) *roseicollis*. A combination of the Pastel and the Ino factors.

Gray Pastel *roseicollis.* This variety is not very distinct from ordinary Pastel. Close inspection reveals a finely variegated lack of pigmentation, a lacy silk-screen pattern that is mainly visible in the mantle and on the back.

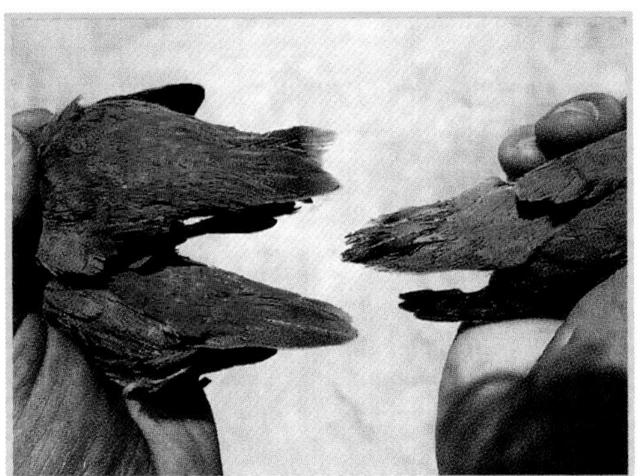

In Pastel *roseicollis*, the expression of factors that affect structural coloration is most evident on the rump. Upper left, Danish Violet Pastel (one factor). Lower left, Cobalt Pastel (one Dark factor). Right, Pastel (no structural factors).

Whiteface Dark Pastel Cinnamon (Whiteface Cinnamon Mauve) *roseicollis*.

Danish Violet Cobalt (Violet Medium Pastel) *roseicollis*. The interaction between one Dark factor and one Danish Violet factor results in a stronger Violet shade.

Pastel *roseicollis*. An incomplete melanin dilution is caused by the Pastel factor. The remaining melanin pigment is responsible for the greenish appearance. This is not a blue bird but a very diluted Green; thus the term Blue must be avoided.

As several mutations will shortly be discussed in which the Pastel factor will appear as one element of a combination, it is not necessary to give further examples of it here.

THE AMERICAN PIED FACTOR

Synonym: Pied.

The Pied is one of the most popular mutations. It may have appeared about 1930 in the USA, but some authors refer to 1960 as the probable date of its appearance.

This factor produces an irregular lack of melanin, so that the birds are pied irregularly. Birds are more yellow or cream pied according to the existing melanin concentration; they can also manifest the character differently, varying from 0% to 100%. The least-pied birds can hardly be distinguished from true normals, which have no Pied factor; however, in general such birds have at least one pied claw. We can call these birds "light Pieds."

Pied Dark Green (Pied Olive) *roseicollis*.

Pied Dark American Yellow (Pied Olive American Yellow) *roseicollis*. Here you can identify the double Dark factor by the slightly gray-tinged rump.

The "heavy Pied" birds are approximately 100% pied and may be totally yellow or cream colored (Buttermilk, according to British usage). They are often very similar to Inos, apart from having black eyes and a blue rump. In

Pied Cobalt Pastel (Medium Pastel) *roseicollis*.

this respect they can be confused with American Yellows (green rumped) or Australian Inos (Australian Cinnamons), which are less bright. Heavy Pieds can be easily obtained through selection. Pairings among heavy Pieds increases the frequency of heavy Pied birds, but it is still possible to get light Pieds from a heavy Pied pair; similarly, a light Pied pair can produce heavy Pied birds.

The Pied factor also causes a dilution of the ground color and gives a snowy shading to the rose-pink color of the forehead and throat. The rose mask is also shortened by the Pied factor, and there is generally a sharp demarcation between the throat and upper breast. In many instances this pattern is the only clue to the presence of the Pied factor in combinations in which it isn't visible (Pied Lutino, for example). The Pied Lutino is usually very difficult to distinguish from a non-Pied Lutino bird; but to trained eyes the first will have a snowy rose mask, shorter and sharply interrupted at the throat and upper breast border, instead of a bright rose-pink mask suffused onto the upper breast, as found on the non-Pied Lutino.

Pieds are very strong birds and can be used to increase the genetic vigor of other mutations through combinations. The chicks

Pied Apple Green *roseicollis*.

Pied Danish Violet Whiteface Cobalt *roseicollis*. Single Dark and Violet factors.

Pied Danish Violet Whiteface Cobalt *roseicollis*. (Back view).

are easily identified while still in the nest, as they have a brighter orange down than the non-Pieds. The beak is either white or light ochre, barely tinged with black at the base, and the first growth in the feather follicles will give an overall pied look to the skin. This is because the differences in melanin concentration are easily seen through the thin, almost transparent skin of the young.

A quantitative aspect is intrinsic to the Pied factor. According to the author's experience, the great majority (75%) of light Pieds (less than 40% of the body pied) will be female. This may point to an interaction with the W chromosome in the population studied.

Being an autosomal dominant, the Pied factor is represented here by *P*, and its normal allele, denoting its absence, as *p*. As it is a dominant gene, only one factor will suffice to produce a Pied phenotype: *pp*—non-Pied; *Pp*—single Pied factor (1F, split for non-Pied); *PP*—double Pied factor (2F). (We represent only the genes in question, which is valid for any combination.)

Some examples:

1. Pied-1F x Pied-1F = 50% Pied-1F; 25% Pied-2F; 25% non-Pied.

2. Pied-2F x Pied-1F = 50% Pied-1F; 50% Pied-2F.

3. Pied-1F x non-Pied = 50% Pied-1F; 50% non-Pied.

Although one of the most widespread mutations in the world, the Pied factor continues to raise doubts about its genetic behavior. Let's consider some of

A heavily Pied Danish Violet Dark American Cinnamon *roseicollis*. The Violet factor spreads a violet shade over the gray (double-factor) rump and enhances the contrast among the Pied, Dark, and Cinnamon factors.

the observations: *(1)* The melanin deficits are randomly located on the bird's body, including claws, skin, and eyes. *(2)* These "marks" can cover from 0 to 100% of the body. *(3)* Heavy Pied birds can be selected by pairings; however, two heavy Pieds can produce a light Pied. *(4)* Two light Pieds can produce a heavy Pied, and new pied marks will appear on the chicks' bodies without conforming to their parents' pied pattern. For example, unpied-tailed birds will generate pied-tailed birds. *(5)* It is said that is very difficult to get double-factored Pied birds (Brockmann and Lantermann 1985), and even a lethal aspect has been suggested (Brockmann 1981). The author's experience confirms the difficulties in getting double-factored Pieds. *(6)*

Orangeface Pied *roseicollis*. A lightly pied bird.

Pied Orangeface Dark Green (olive) *roseicollis*.

Sometimes supposed double-factor birds produce a non-Pied bird.

To try to explain these phenomena genetically, we have to go beyond Mendelism and get into molecular genetics. Genes are formed, as you know, by DNA or RNA sequences, which function like computer programs, and any error during their replication may appear as a mutation. In order to prevent very frequent mutations, there are mechanisms in the processes of cell division (meiosis and mitosis) to correct these errors. We have seen before that mutant phenotypes are due to the these errors, leading in this case to a pied bird. It probably effectively inhibits melanin synthesis because it makes formation of one or more of its generative enzymes impossible.

The percentage of successful corrections of these errors which are responsible for the Pied phenotype is inversely proportional to the number of pied marks. So these pied marks would appear in cell lines where these "correctors" didn't act. Such a mechanism acts as a real "pointer," or "setter," of marks and would have maximal effect during mitotic divisions in embryo genesis. This correction mechanism can and does have a genetic component, as we can select heavy Pied birds through pairings.

Genetically, the Pieds are in fact mosaics. This view offers a reasonable explanation for what so far we have supposed to be an absence of double-factored birds. But double-factor Pieds do occur, and probably with a Mendelian frequency. The fact that light Pieds or normals (non-Pied) may appear from a double-factored pair is possibly due to the action of correction mechanisms during meiosis, when the gametes are formed. That is, there are different cell lines in mosaicism.

Australian Yellow *roseicollis*, the rare Pied phase. Such birds can be selected; however, some that are pied initially will in time lose their markings and become wholly yellow.

Pied single-factor Danish Violet Whiteface Cobalt (Medium) *roseicollis*.

You can conceptualize this in the following fashion: there are Pied-marked feathers in one bird; these Pied markings have their source in the bird's gametes (spermatozoon or ovum). This means the gamete might be a spermatozoon or ovum both with and without Pied factors, as a mosaic in a double-factor bird. This also explains the existence of dilute Pied birds; there can also be Green birds that contain the

Pied factor mosaically in their gametes.

How do you introduce the Pied factor into other colors? Nothing could be easier, as we can see in the following example for Pastel Pied, which is nothing but the combination of the Pied and the Pastel factors, that is, *Ppyy* or *PPyy*.

1. Pastel x Pied-1F Green = Pied-1F Green /Pastel; Green / Pastel.

2. Pastel x Pied-1F Green / Pastel = Pied-1F Green /Pastel; Pastel; Green /Pastel; Pastel Pied-1F.

3. Pastel Pied-1F x Pastel = Pastel Pied-1F; Pastel.

To obtain any other Pied combination, just follow the above examples, substituting the chosen factor for the Pastel factor (there will be some exceptions when dealing with sex-linked factors).

THE RED-EYE FACTOR

We are not sure whether a Red-eye factor that is not an Ino factor exists. However, there are red-eyed birds for which inheritance is autosomal. All the birds in question were light Pieds. There may be a link between the Red-eye factor and the Pied factor. Another doubt still remains: is the Red-eye factor independent of the Pied factor? It could be nothing more than an example of mosaicism: a bird without melanin in the retinal cells, or, put another way, a bird pied in the eyes. No doubt, a lot of research needs to be done to correctly explain this supposed Red-eye factor!

Orangeface Australian Yellow *roseicollis*. here the summative action of two diluting factors produces a bright yellow bird with red eyes. The totally yellow rump and primaries indicate that this is not an Ino.

THE DARK FACTOR

The Dark factor appeared in Germany. It is undoubtedly one of the most important in the color combinations of agapornism.

This factor does not produce any color itself; instead, it darkens the ground color to which is added. It alters the cloudy zone, making it thinner. This increases the light absorbed by the medulla, darkening the whole phenotype. Different levels of darkening occur, according to the number of genes involved. The Dark factor acts as an incompletely dominant quantitative gene.

Often, the thinner cloudy zone

Dark Apple Green Australian Yellow *roseicollis*. The overall yellow color is the result of one Whiteface factor; the dark grayish shade on the back and rump signifies the presence of two Dark factors.

results in such distinct phenotypes that they are readily named according to their appearance: *(1)* Green heterozygote for Dark factor: Medium Green, or Jade. *(2)* Pastel heterozygote for Dark factor: = Medium Pastel, or Cobalt. *(3)* Green homozygote for Dark factor: Dark Green, or Olive. *(4)* Pastel homozygote for Dark factor: Dark Pastel, or Mauve, or Slate.

This way, the linguistic terms accord with the genetic situation. If we have a Green bird (not Pastel or Whiteface), it will receive the term *Medium*, or *Jade*. For example: Cinnamon Green heterozygous for the Dark factor = Jade Cinnamon, or Medium Green Cinnamon.

Every non-yellow bird (Pastel, Whiteface) will receive the term *Medium*, or *Cobalt*. *Medium* in this context is often used only with the term *Blue* (e.g, Medium Blue). As we have chosen the term *Pastel*, it seems more appropriate to use *Cobalt*. So we have Cinnamon Pastel heterozygous for the Dark factor = Cobalt Cinnamon, or Medium Pastel Cinnamon. Pied Pastel

Dark Apple Green American Yellow *roseicollis*. The salmon pink on the face (instead of the normal rose pink) establishes this bird as an Apple Green. The double Dark factor is evident in the gray rump and the dark marbling of the wing coverts.

Orangeface Dark Green (Olive) *roseicollis*.

heterozygous for the Dark factor = Pied Cobalt; etc.

The terms *Olive* for yellows and *Mauve* or *Slate* for non-yellows are used similarly when the Dark factor is homozygous. The term *Dark* is also used for homozygous birds: Dark Green = Olive; Dark Cinnamon = Cinnamon Olive; Dark Pastel = Mauve, or Slate; Dark Pastel Cinnamon = Cinnamon Mauve, or Cinnamon Slate.

The Pastel factor is linked to the Dark factor; when they are put together, their inheritance patterns won't follow the Mendelian expectations. (Example 6). In general, there is a darkening of the phenotype of such birds, and the rump will turn into gray in double Dark-factored birds. Pairings can be modelled on Example 8, which covers the great majority of cases. However, we can notice differences among the Medium Green phenotypes: some are darker, while others are very light and even indistinguishable from normals—yet they will produce double Dark-factored birds (Dark Greens, or Olives). The same phenomenon occurs in Pastel (non-yellow) bloodlines. It had already attracted the attention of various authors, along with the existence of different color tones

Orangeface Medium Green American Cinnamon *roseicollis* (one Dark factor).

in Olives and Slates. This situation was explained by the author and a colleague (D'Angieri and Oliveira 1989b).

The Dark factor in actuality is a group formed by three pairs of genes, polymeric and quantitatively inherited. The Dark complex consists of the following three Dark genes *E1*, *E2*, and *E3*. together with their normal (non-Dark) alleles *e1*, *e2*, and *e3*. Each of these mutant genes is responsible for a certain percentage of cloudy-zone narrowing: *E1*—12%, light phenotype; *E2*—16%, intermediate phenotype; *E3*—22%, dark phenotype. (These percentage values are estimations for purposes of illustration.) All of these phenotypes are heterozygotes, i.e., *E1* = light Medium Green; *E2* = intermediate Medium Green; and *E3* = dark Medium Green. In a Pastel strain, Cobalts would follow the same pattern.

Dark Apple Green American Cinnamon *roseicollis*. You can see the greenish brown shade produced by the Whiteface factor.

Orangeface Dark Green American Cinnamon *roseicollis*.

The phenotypes previously called Dark (Olives, Mauves, etc.) occur after a certain percentage of cloudy-zone narrowing. It must be narrowed about 28% for the bird to appear a light Olive (light Dark Green).

Ranked in terms of decreasing frequency, the incidence of Dark genes at present is *E2*, *E1*, and *E3* (D'Angieri and Oliveira 1989b). All

Orangeface Dark Green Australian Cinnamon *roseicollis*.

are linked (otherwise, we could obtain Green birds from an Olive pair), and the rate of crossing over is nearly 0%.

Some examples:

1. E1e2e3 /e1E2e3; e1e2e3 / E1E2e3 = 28–32% narrowed: light Dark Green (light Olive) or light Dark Pastel (light Mauve).

2. E1e2e3 /E1E2e3; e1E2E3 / e1e2e3; E1e2e3 /e1e2E3 = 32–40% narrowed: medium Olive or Mauve.

3. e1E2e3 /E1e2E3; etc. = more than 40% narrowed: dark Olive (Dark Green) or Mauve (Dark Pastel).

The possible combinations are most variable when you use all three Dark gene pairs, despite the limitations due to low crossover rates.

Exhaustive work has been done in order to obtain a maximal narrowing of the cloudy zone, adding as many dark genes as possible, in order to get a triple Dark homozygote *(E1E1E2E2E3E3)*, which phenotypically would be a nearly black lovebird. For ordinary, day-to-day pairings, it is sufficient to figure with only one pair of Dark genes, as we estimate that about 90% of the Dark-factored birds are *E2*.

THE AMERICAN YELLOW FACTOR

Synonyms: American Golden Cherryhead, American Dilute.

The name itself describes this

Double-factor Violet Cobalt (double-factor Violet Medium Pastel) *roseicollis*. Here we can see the strong darkening produced when two Danish Violet factors are present. There is also one Dark factor present here.

Medium green *roseicollis* with E2 Dark factor (left) and E3 Dark factor (right). The difference is quite subtle, being seen mainly on the wing coverts and nape and around the ear coverts. E3 is a little bit darker.

factor. It produces a bright ochre yellow lovebird, with a golden suffusion and a characteristic marbled pattern on the wing coverts. It is inherited as an autosomal recessive. A melanin diluter, it also may change the feather structure and is easily detectable in combinations. It can be combined with all the *roseicollis* mutations, most commonly with the Pastel factor.

This gene locus has multiple alleles; the other is the Graywing factor.

Pastel American Yellow. Synonyms: Silver Cherryhead, White.

The combination called Silver is

Orangeface American Yellow *roseicollis*.

American Yellow *roseicollis*.

The marbled wing coverts are typical of this mutation.

in truth a grayish lemon-colored lovebird which is produced by the partial lack of psittacin due to the Pastel factor and of melanin due to the American Yellow factor; its genotype is *aayy* (Example 4).

Observations: Several combinations are really beautiful (Cinnamon American Yellow and Whiteface American Yellow, for example). One very interesting combination involves American Yellow and Australian Lutino (Australian Cinnamon); it could be called American Yellow Australian Lutino. It resembles American

American Yellow Australian Ino *roseicollis*. The interaction of these two melanin-diluting factors produces a bird that looks very similar to a Lutino. However, the gray-barred tail feathers and the slightly gray primaries show that it is not a Lutino.

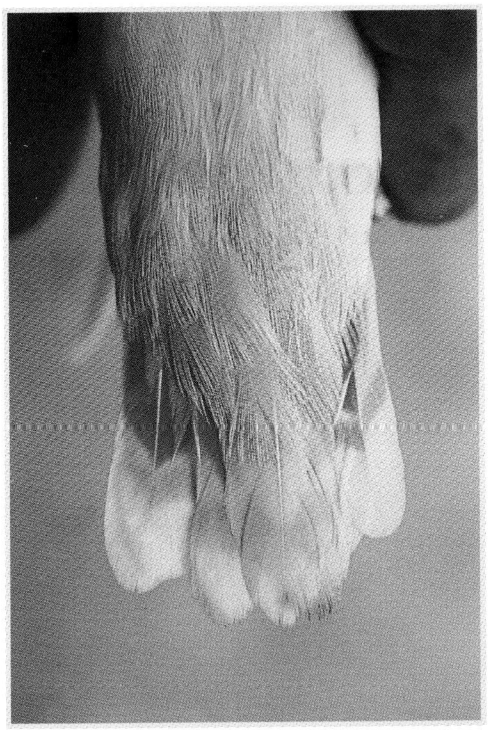

American Yellow Australian Ino *roseicollis*. The slightly bluish rump and gray-barred tail feathers are characteristic of this combination, and serve to distinguish it from the American Lutino.

Whiteface Graywing Cobalt *roseicollis*.

Lutino, having red eyes but with the American Yellow's rump. This phenotype is quite obvious, as we are diluting a partial lutinism, making it closer to a total lutino (see Ino factor).

THE GRAYWING FACTOR

This is an autosomal recessive character, which is not well expressed in *agapornis*. Originating in America, at the present time it is not widespread. This is a yellowish dilute green bird, very similar to an American Yellow but darker and with gray wings. The wing coverts are marbled with a gray shade.

Birds called Silver (Graywing American White) are greenish blue with yellowish marbled wing coverts.

The allele of Graywing, American Yellow, is recessive to it. Thus Graywings mated with American Yellows will produce 100% Graywings. This is another good example in *Agapornis* of polyallelia: two different mutant genes at the same locus. Double-factored Graywing birds are distinctive: more gray, with a stronger gray marbling on the wings. Generally, double-factored birds are males, a fact that still remains to be explained.

THE JAPANESE YELLOW FACTOR

Synonym: Japanese Golden Cherryhead.

Graywing American White. With the Graywing factor there is a greenish shade on the body and a bright silver gray color in the primaries. The wing coverts retain the marbled yellowish color. This combination is quite beautiful.

The name indicates its country of origin; one of the most beautiful mutations, it appeared in Japan in the aviaries of Mr. Masaru Iwata, about 1950. This lovebird is a bright yellow with an almost metallic luster. Thus the Japanese spoke of it as the Imperial Japanese Golden Cherryhead Peach-face Lovebird. The "Golden Cherry" part was erroneously applied to several other mutations.

This mutation causes a structural alteration in the cloudy zone that neutralizes the optical effects that are responsible for the visible blue color. We have here a not-blue lovebird, but some greenish blue tinge is still present due to interference.

Japanese Yellow is an autosomal recessive. It can be combined with several other factors, notably Dark and Pastel. The latter, in the author's opinion, produces the most beautiful combination in agapornism.

Japanese Yellow *roseicollis*. The color is quite uniform, with a structural pattern that shows a reflection like that from the surface of water.

Japanese Yellow Pastel. This combination, also called Japanese Silver Cherry, was imagined to be an almost snow-white lovebird, as a result of the combination of a structurally non-blue and a non-yellow; that is, without pigmentation. In fact, this does not occur, as the Pastel factor doesn't remove all the carotenoids (remember, there is no Blue in *roseicollis*).

N.B.: The Japanese Yellow, unhappily, is a pleiotropic factor, responsible for an associated deleterious character: all homozygotic females have a problem with calcium absorption and synthesis, so their eggs are soft, with a very thin shell, or even shell-less. The only birds suitable for breeding are split females (heterozygotes for Japanese Yellow).

THE INO FACTOR

In *roseicollis*, the Ino factor encompasses two alleles, both recessive and sex linked (they are found on the Z chromosome). One allele is responsible for the Lutino phenotype, the other is Australian Ino. The latter phenotype exhibits a partial lutinism and was erroneously called Australian Cinnamon; such a partial schizochroism should be termed Australian Ino.

Lutino. A Lutino first appeared in 1973 in Mrs. Mabel Schertzer's aviaries in San Diego, California. Quite properly, it is considered to be one of the most beautiful *roseicollis* mutations. It is a golden yellow lovebird, with primaries and rump white; the feet, claws, and beak are pink salmon, and the eyes red.

Orangeface American Lutino *roseicollis*. Note the white rump and primaries.

This American Ino factor is recessive and sex-linked, which means that it's totally impossible for female birds to be split for Ino. If a female possesses this Ino factor, it is a Lutino. (There is just one exception with Lacewings, treated below).

There are not many combinations involving the American Ino factor that can be recommended: it is epistatic to the great majority of the other mutant genes, which are therefore not visible in combinations. Dark Green (Olive) Lutinos, for example, are practically indistinguishable from Lutinos without Dark factors—but these birds can be used as Dark-factor introducers:

1. Lutino male x Olive Lutino female = 100% Jade Lutinos.

2. Olive Lutino male x Olive female = 100% Olive / Lutino males; 100% Olive Lutino females.

3. Olive / Lutino male x Olive Lutino female = Olive and Olive Lutinos (males and females).

The above examples are a curiosity, but they can be useful in certain pairings with Australian Inos and others.

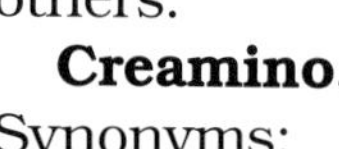

Creamino. Synonyms: Albino, Pastel Ino.

The most common combination involving the American Ino is the Pastel Ino, more commonly called Creamino, or Albino. The term *Albino* is not correct, as it signifies a totally unpigmented bird. We all know that this is not true of this variety. Creaminos combine the Pastel factor with the American Ino factor. They are a milky cream color, with red eyes and salmon pink feet.

Orangeface Australian Ino (Orangeface Australian Cinnamon)*roseicollis*.

They can be obtained like this:

Lutino male (ZiZiYY) x Pastel female (ZIWyy).

	ZiY	ZiY
ZIy	ZIZiYy	ZIZiYy
Wy	ZiWYy	ZiWYy

50% Green /Ino /Pastel males (ZIZiYy); 50% Lutino /Pastel females (ZiWYy).

Pairing these together: ZIZiYy x ZiWYy.

	ZiY	Ziy	WY	Wy
ZIY	ZIZiYY	ZIZiYy	ZIWYY	ZIWYy
ZIy	ZIZiYy	ZIZiyy	ZIWYy	ZIWyy
ZiY	ZiZiYY	ZiZiYy	ZiWYY	ZiWYy
Ziy	ZiZiYy	ZiZiyy	ZiWYy	ZiWyy

1/16 Green /Ino male (ZIZiYY).
2/16 Green /Ino /Pastel male (ZIZiYy).
1/16 Pastel /Ino male (ZIZiyy).
1/16 Lutino male (ZiZiYY).
2/16 Lutino /Pastel male (ZiZiYy).
1/16 Creamino male (ZiZiyy).
1/16 Green female (ZIWYY).
2/16 Green /Pastel female (ZIWYy).
1/16 Pastel female (ZIWyy).
1/16 Lutino female (ZiWYY).
2/16 Lutino /Pastel female (ZiWYy).
1/16 Creamino female (ZiWyy).

Thus twelve genotypes result, yielding four different phenotypes: Green, Pastel, Lutino, and Creamino (Pastel Ino).

Orangeface Creamino *roseicollis*.

Whiteface Ino. Synonym: Whiteface Albino.

The name reflects the combination: Whiteface factor and American Ino factor. This lovebird is very similar to the Creamino, but it has a more yellowish back and a white face. Its breast is almost totally white, only slightly tinged with blue. To produce this combination, just substitute Whiteface in place of Pastel in Example 9.

Apple Green Lutino. This is a double heterozygote for Pastel and Whiteface, combined with American Ino.

THE AUSTRALIAN INO FACTOR

One of the most beautiful examples of the Ino factor appeared in Mr. R. Fisk's aviaries in Sidney, Australia. It is a yellow lovebird very slightly tinged with green, with a blue rump, gray primaries, and purple irises. This sex-linked factor was at first taken to be a Cinnamon-series mutation. Certainly it is not a cinnamon bird, but today it is still known as Australian Cinnamon.

From Australia this mutation spread widely, and several marvelous combinations were produced. When the American Ino factor was added, the results were surprising: the Australian showed itself dominant to American Ino. Several studies subsequently explained its inheritance definitively (D'Angieri 1987).

This mutation is in fact a partial schizochroism (partial lutinism, in this case), and *not* a cinnamon. It is a mutation of the same gene responsible for American Ino, and it occurred independently. It produces a higher melanin concentration than its American allele.

These two genes are the first recorded case of polyallelia in *Agapornis* (D'Angieri 1987). The correct appellation should be Australian Lutino—not quite perfect but, without doubt, more correct than the Cinnamon that is still very widely used. Its inheritance is identical to American Ino; just substitute the gene *i* with *ia* in the previous examples.

Mustard. Synonyms: Olive Australian Lutino, Olive

Double factored Violet Cobalt (Doubled factored Violet Medium Pastel). Here we can see the strong darkening promoved by the Violet shade in when two Danish Violet factors are present. There is also one Dark factor involved here.

Australian Cinnamon, Dark Australian Lutino, Dark Australian Cinnamon.

The combinations with the Australian Ino are very gratifying, as it is not so epistatic as its American allele. Thus Olive Australian Lutino—called Mustard by Australians—is a visible, and pretty, combination. To produce it, just use the Australian allele in the Olive Lutino example above. With Australian Ino factor = *Zia*, and *En* = any one of the Dark-factor alleles: Mustard males have the genotype *EnEnZiaZia*, while females are *EnEnZiaW*.

Ivory Synonyms: Australian Creamino, Australian Pastelino, Australian Cinnamon Pastel, Blue Australian Cinnamon.

Ivory is the Australian name, and also is appropriate in that this combination is perfectly described: ivory color, gray primaries, blue rump, and dark purple eyes.

It is produced by combining the Pastel and Australian Ino factors (Example 9, which shows its allele, is analogous).

Whiteface Ivory. Analogous to Whiteface Ino, this is a combination of the Whiteface factor (homozygote) and the Australian Ino factor. If the Whiteface factor is heterozygous, we have Australian Apple Green Lutino.

Cobalt Ivory and Mauve Ivory. Synonyms: Australian Mauve Creamino, Cobalt Australian Creamino, Cobalt Australian Cinnamon.

These very interesting combinations, attractive and useful, can be gotten simply by adding Dark factors to the Ivory above: one Dark factor makes Cobalt Ivory, two Dark factors produce Mauve, or Slate Ivory.

THE AMERICAN CINNAMON FACTOR

This mutation appeared in the USA in the seventies. Laymen can see immediately that it is overall not a cinnamon bird, but a slightly ochre light green. The vanes and shafts of the primaries are cinnamon brown, and it has pink claws and purple eyes, with the iris light cinnamon. The purple eyes are especially evident in chicks, which have a brownish beak with a black base. The down is bright orange due to the carotenoids present.

The appearance results from a dilution in melanin concentration, in which case the phaeomelanin predominates—which itself is nothing but a smaller concentration of melanin pigment, in smaller granules.

The addition of this factor to others will cause a dilution in them, giving a brighter appearance along with a cinnamon rachis. When the Pied factor is present, there will be a suffusion of the Pied marks, resulting in a quite uniform bright yellow coloration.

The Cinnamon factor is recessive and sex linked, which means it is on the Z chromosome. Thus we can say there are no females heterozygous (split) for American Cinnamon; they are either Cinnamon or not (Lacewing females are an exception). Heterozygote birds (splits) can

American Cinnamon *roseicollis*.

only be males and can be found in any ground color. Split birds (heterozygotes for Cinnamon) can be identified by a cinnamon cast on the border between the rose-pink mask and the upper breast. This is easily seen in Greens and Pastel birds but very difficult to detect in yellows (Inos, American Yellows, etc.).

Examples, where *ZcZc* = Cinnamon male and *ZcW* = Cinnamon female:

1. Cinnamon male x Cinnamon female = 100% Cinnamon (males and females).

2. Cinnamon male x Green female = 100% Green /Cinnamon males and 100% Cinnamon females.

3. Green /Cinnamon male x Cinnamon female = 50% Cinnamon males and females; 25% Green /Cinnamon males; 25% Green females.

Cinnamon Pastel. Synonyms: Cinnamon Blue, Blue Cinnamon, Cinnamon Pastel Blue.

This is a combination of Cinnamon, *Zc*, and Pastel, *y*, which results in a Cinnamon bird with a Pastel ground color.

Paster x American Cinnamon

ZZyy

	Zy	Zy
Z^cY	Z^cZYy	Z^cZYy
WY	ZWYy	ZWYy

By following this example, you can produce several combinations with the American Cinnamon factor.

Lacewing Factor. Synonyms: Cinnamon Ino.

The Lacewings are very interesting lovebirds, being a combination of American Cinnamon and any of the Ino factors (either American or Australian). The name *Lacewing* came from a combination of mutations in the Budgerigar (*Melopsittacus undulatus*), which is a bird with barred wings. The expectation of getting something similar in lovebirds was frustrated. American Lacewings (that is, the combination of the Cinnamon factor with the American Ino) are yellow, slightly tinged with green on the wing coverts, a bluish rump, and red eyes—very similar to the American Yellow Australian Lutino (Golden Australian Lutino).

Lutino x American Cinnamon

Z^{iC} Z^{iC}

	Z^{ic}	Z^{ic}
Z^{ic}	Z^{iC} Z^{ic}	Z^{iC} Z^{Ic}
W	$Z^{iC}W$	$Z^{iC}W$

Let's examine the following pairing: Lutino male (ZiCZiC) x Amer. Cinnamon female (ZIcW). The result is 50% Green /Ino / Cinnamon males (ZiCZIc) and 50% Lutino females (ZiCW). During gametogenesis, duplication of the chromatids occurs, with the possibility of crossing-over. In order to have Lacewings, it is necessary to get the genes i (Ino) and c (Cinnamon) onto the same chromatid (chromosome filament). ZiCZIc offers the following crossover possibilities: ZIC, ZIc, ZiC, and Zic. Theoretically, supposing a maximal crossover rate, we should have gametes formed at a rate of 25% each. This doesn't occur in fact; getting Lacewing is quite difficult, because the Z chromosome is small, and so the Ino and Cinnamon factors are very close to one another. Additionally, after the zygote ZicZic is formed, crossing-over may occur again, undoing the Lacewing combination. Therefore, the real rate for Lacewing is 3.25%. If Lacewings are not paired correctly, they can disappear.

THE FALLOW FACTOR

The Fallow mutation, also called Fawn, is a fawn schizochroism, for which there are two distinct mutations: one appeared in East Germany in 1977, the other in West Germany in 1978. The mutations were named according to their provenance, and though nowadays the two Germanies are unified, here we are going keep these names.

Some breeders doubt that the East German Fallow is a distinct mutation. Yet there is a quite perceptible difference between their phenotypes: Eastern Fallows are lighter and quite similar to an Australian Lutino. Both mutations cause a partial absence of eumelanin (black melanin), so the phaeomelanin (brown melanin) predominates here. The lack of eumelanin is greater in the East German Fallow. Fallows are in general similar to American Cinnamons, but have red eyes and are more brownish.

West German Fallow. This mutation appeared in West Germany in Mr. Bodo Ochs's aviaries. So far it is not very widespread. This bloodline was not developed by Mr. Ochs; it was separated into two flocks; one went to Holland and the other to Brazil. In Holland this mutation is quite well established but not abundant; in Brazil it continues to be very rare.

As with all new mutations, this one presents several problems: lethal genes, susceptibility to diseases due to inbreeding, etc. The Fallows have been shown to be very sensitive to a minimal degree of inbreeding, to influenza, and to climatic changes. This weakness, fortunately, was overcome, opening of a whole field of additional combinations in agapornism.

The author's experience suggests you avoid inbreeding with Fallow bloodlines. Fallow is an autosomal recessive, and so far it has followed the Mendelian laws.

Green x Fallow (FF x ff) yields 100% Green /Fallow (Ff). Pairing the offspring (Ff x Ff) produces 25% Green (FF), 50% Green / Fallow (Ff), and 25% Fallow (ff).

Example 18: Let's see now how to get Pastel Fallows: Pastel x Fallow (FFyy x ffYY) produces 100% Green /Fallow /Pastel (FfYy). Next, put these together: FfYy x FfYy.

	FY	Fy	fY	fy
FY	FFYY	FFYy	FfYY	FfYy
Fy	FFYy	FFyy	FfYy	Ffyy
fY	FfYY	FfYy	ffYY	ffYy
fy	FfYy	Ffyy	ffYy	ffyy

Of the possible offspring, 1/16 will be Pastel Fallow (ffyy).

East German Fallow. This is a very rare and valuable mutation, unknown to many breeders and disputed by others. It has a smaller concentration of eumelanin than its Western counterpart, and so is like an Australian Lutino with red eyes. It is autosomal recessive and completely distinct from Western Fallow. Pairing Eastern Fallows *f2* with Western fallows *f* will produce 100% Green (wild phenotype) lovebirds, which proves these factors are totally distinct. These Greens are heterozygous for both mutations, and theoretically could produce a double Fallow *fff2f2*, but we haven't seen such a bird so far.

You can examine its inheritance by using the table for West German Fallow, using *f2* instead of *f*.

THE DANISH VIOLET FACTOR

The Danish Violet, as you might suppose, came from Denmark. A structural mutation, it doesn't directly change the amount of pigmentation. This fact suggests a possible similarity to the Dark complex: in combinations it will produce a wide variety of phenotypes, all tinged with a violet shade. We are careful here to use the expression *violet shade*, as that is what really happens to the phenotypes to which the Violet factor is added.

The violet shade seems due to the action of an autosomal incompletely dominant gene that enlarges the feather barbs and the diameter of the medulla. This increases the absorption of light rays having a wavelength greater than 420 nm. The short-wavelength light rays are

Double-factor Violet American Cinnamon *roseicollis*. The darkening is the result of homozygosity (two factors) for Danish Violet; there is no Dark factor involved in this bird. The lilac rump is due to interaction between the Cinnamon and the Violet factors.

Green East German Fallow *roseicollis*. This variety can be identified by its blue rump and red eyes.

Danish Violet Whiteface Australian Ino *roseicollis*.

unaffected by this phenomenon, and the outcome, influenced further by the cloudy zone, is an increase in the visibity of light rays from the violet spectrum (420–380 nm.). Carotenoids when present can some what alter the violet color, but in general a violet shading covers the entire body, being much more pronounced in non-yellow birds.

This violet shade effectively darkens the phenotype, especially the rump. It changes into a strong violet, which is perfectly visible in all ground colors except in double Dark-factored birds (it depends on which type *E* is involved).

Violet Cobalts are the best example of the sum of two darkening factors (Dark and Violet), yet this additive effect makes it very difficult to produce distinctive Violet Mauves. Dark-factor homozygosity can cause a very extensive light absorption that can be epistatic to the violet factor. But it will occur only when *E2* and *E3* are involved; Dark factor type *E1* is not strong enough to mask the violet shade; so we have patent Mauve (Dark Pastel) Danish Violets when the E1 Dark factor is involved. The author has had the opportunity to demonstrate through selected pairings that there will be three different Violet Mauves, depending on which of the Dark factors is involved (*E1, E2, E3*).

Danish Violet Whiteface American White *roseicollis*. One Violet factor.

Danish Violet *Green roseicollis*. The double-factor form is a quite dark bird with a deep violet blue tinge. It is important to note that the Dark factor is not involved here.

Danish Violet Medium Apple Green *roseicollis*. Only one Violet factor is involved here, together with one Dark factor, one Pastel, and one White-face factor. Whiteface-factored birds will show a softened Violet effect.

Danish Violet Cobalt (Danish Violet Medium Pastel).

Danish Violet American Cinnamon *roseicollis*. On the left, the rump of a single-factor Violet bird; on the right, double factor. A second Violet factor intensifies the lilac color on the rump and also darkens the plumage overall.

Danish Violet Whiteface Cobalt *roseicollis*. Single Dark and Violet factors.

Double-factor Danish Violet Apple Green *roseicollis*. Addition of a second Violet factor darkens the overall appearance considerably.

Pied Dark Pastel. A combination between American pied factor and dark factor (homo zigote) and pastel factor.

THE AMERICAN VIOLET FACTOR

The American Violet factor has an action similar to that of its Danish analogue, but its expressivity is quite different. American Violet is most visible as Cobalt Whiteface Violet. In Pastel birds it is slightly visible, while in another combinations it is hypostatic (the character isn't manifest).

The author doesn't know how the American and the Danish Violets are related. They may be alleles or may constitute a Violet complex similar to the Dark complex; or perhaps American Violet is a fourth type of Dark factor.

THE AUSTRALIAN YELLOW FACTOR

Synonym: Australian Golden Cherry.

This mutation appeared for the first time in Mr. Ron Fisk's aviaries in Australia. It is a melanin diluter that manifests itself as a totally yellow bird with a snowy rose-pink forehead, throat, and upper breast, and with black eyes. The border dividing the mask and the breast is well demarcated, as in American Pied. The rump varies in coloration from a mossy green to totally yellow. Sometimes this green rump color suffuses onto the back toward the mantle and nape, giving this bird a Pied look. This peculiarity made Mr. Hayward treat this mutation as a "recessive Pied" that is 100% yellow in the great majority of cases. The author considers it prudent not to view them as Pieds, since 99.999% of the time they are totally yellow birds. It is more prudent to consider them as the expression of a melanin diluter gene. No epistatic gene is involved.

American Violet Cobalt (American Violet Medium Pastel) *roseicollis*. This is one of the few phenotypes in which the American Violet factor is visible.

The fact that this mutation is quite similar to heavy American Pied has kept this factor from receiving from breeders much of the attention it deserves; it is often confused with American Pied. Unhappily, as a result of such inadvertence this magnificent and valuable mutation is still rare elsewhere in the world outside of Australia.

Australian Yellows are very

Rump alterations in *roseicollis* with various factors. Upper left, Lutino (white). Lower left, Australian Ino (blue). Right, Australian Yellow (yellow tinged with green).

The only *roseicollis* mutation that produces a sexual dimorphism is the Australian Yellow factor. The male on the left, has a bright yellow rump and rectrices, while the female, on the right, has a much more greenish color in these areas.

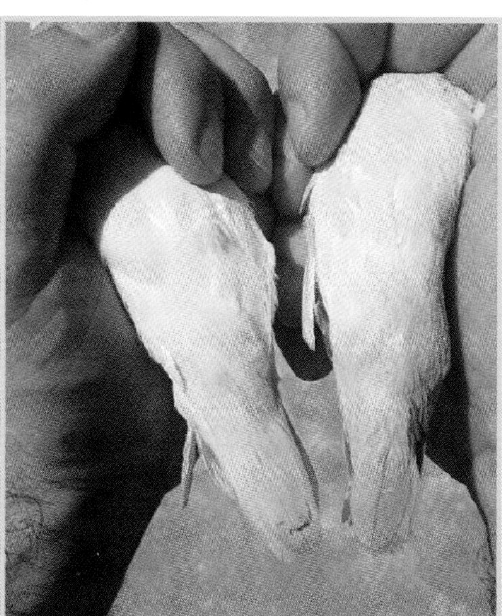

Green birds split for Australian Yellow can be easily identified by a yellow spot on the inner surface of the legs, just above the hock.

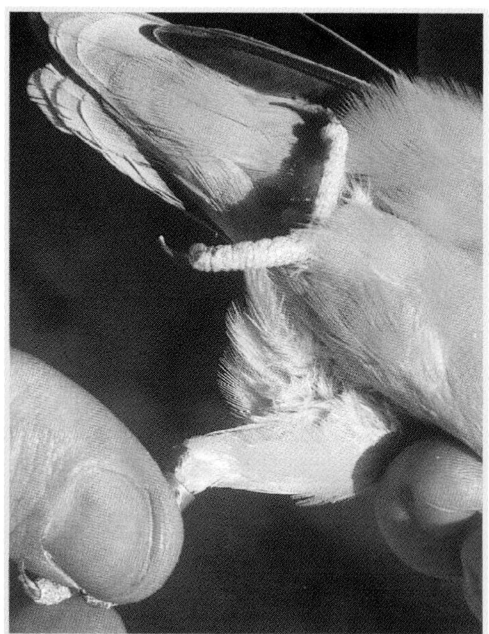

Orangeface Australian Yellow *roseicollis*. Note that the primaries are a light yellow color.

robust lovebirds, and generally very good parents. But they have some behavioral peculiarities: they are shy, calm, and don't fly very much; they generally prefer to walk about, via the netting and perches. This is probably due to alterations in bone structure. They appear to have a lighter bone structure, although they are a little bigger and wider than other lovebirds (a further instance of pleiotropism). This factor is an autosomal recessive, represented as *pr*. It is a perfect example that mutations affect not only coloration but also shape and behavior.

Heterozygotes for Australian Yellow are easily identified in the yellow-ground (Green) birds by a yellow spot in the inside of the thighs. Many combinations can be made, the commonest being with the Pastel factor.

Australian White. Synonyms: Australian Silver Cherry, Australian Pastel Yellow, Primrose.

A rare combination in the Americas and even in Europe, it is very common in Australia, where, due to its beauty, it has been called Primrose. This is a cream bird, usually totally so, with black irises and a rump slightly tinged with green. To get it, model your pairings on Example 4, where its analogue is American Silver.

THE WHITEFACE FACTOR

The Whiteface factor is an autosomal recessive that gives us a phenotype in which a partial absence of carotenoids (psittacin) occurs. This absence is greater than with the Pastel factor. The Whitefaces exhibit a facial mask very poor in psittacin, often totally white, though individuals with a slightly pink forehead can be found, mainly older birds. The body is a purer blue than is found among Pastels. Principally the breast, back, mantle, and nape are a metallic greenish bright blue.

Among many breeders the inheritance of Whiteface still generates controversy, mainly when the Pastel factor is involved, as it is in the great majority of instances. Almost all birds that carry the Whiteface factor are either in the Whiteface or Apple Green form. Apple Greens, unhappily and erroneously, are thought to be Pastels heterozygotic for Whiteface. The true mode of inheritance was fully explained only recently (D'Angieri & Oliveira 1989a).

We must bear in mind that Whiteface and Pastel are two completely distinct factors, not alleles. Both are autosomal recessives that diminish carotenoid pigment (psittacin), but to different levels. As you see, both have a similar action, but White-face is a stronger psittacin diluter. This mechanism permits a summative action (although it is not total) when Pastel and Whiteface are combined; there is some interference between them.

Let's first analyze the commonest phenotype in the Whiteface series, which is also the most susceptible to mistakes: the Apple Green Peach-faced Lovebird. Apple Greens are

Australian Yellow *roseicollis*. There is a characteristic green shade on the back and rump in the Australian Yellow birds.

Whiteface *roseicollis*. Original mutation standard. Front and back views.

Pied Whiteface *roseicollis*.

Medium American White (Yellow Pastel) *roseicollis*.

Medium Ivory *roseicollis*. A single Dark factor is combined with Pastel and Australian Ino.

Whiteface Pastel *roseicollis*. Double Whiteface and double Pastel factors. The opacity of the color on the back and the breast distinguish this combination from the simple Whiteface; there is no metallic reflection, and the Whiteface markings are absent.

heterozygotic for both Pastel and Whiteface; i.e., they are splits for both factors. The summative action of the genes produces a dilute-colored bird of an apple green color with a salmon forehead and facial mask. This bird is *not* a blue-series bird but a Green in which two psittacin-diluter genes which are not alleles are present in a heterozygous condition.

The cited factors' interaction produces a phenotypic variability among Whiteface birds; there are some with a more or less white facial mask and even some that are quite similar to Pastels but that give white-faced chicks. Also, a Whiteface pair can generate Pastel-looking young. This confused the minds of breeders for years.

Today we know that Pastel and Whiteface are linked and have a crossover rate of 0.68% (D'Angieri & Oliveira 1989a). This explains perfectly why we get almost only Apple Green, Whiteface, and Pastel in an Apple Green x Apple Green pairing.

Example 19: Whiteface is shown as w, Pastel as y.

Apple Green (YyWw) x Apple Green (YyWw).

	YW	Yw	yW	yw
YW	YYWW	YYWw	YyWW	YyWw
Yw	YYWw	YYww	YyWw	Yyww
yW	YyWW	YyWw	yyWW	yyWw
yw	YyWw	Yyww	yyWw	yyww

So we have:

Green (YYWW).

Green /Pastel (YyWW).

Green /Whiteface (YYWw).

Japanese White *roseicollis.* The extremely uniform coloration makes this combination one of the most attractive in lovebird breeding.

Apple Green (Green /Pastel / Whiteface, YyWw).

Whiteface (YYww).

Whiteface /Pastel (Yyww, forehead slightly tinged with pink).

Pastel /Whiteface (yyWw).

Whiteface Pastel (yyww).

Orangeface Medium Apple Green *roseicollis*.

All phenotypes in this table were obtained by the author, including normal Greens born from a pair of Apple Greens. This mechanism is quite simple if you think of Apple Greens as psittacin-diluted Greens.

THE ORANGEFACE FACTOR

One of the newest *roseicollis* mutations, the Orangeface factor is an incompletely dominant factor that dilutes psittacin to a lower concentration, enough to change the red-pink into an orange color. The green is also altered, becoming brighter and yellowish. There may also be a small structural alteration together with a quasi-quantitative change in the pigments that produces increased scattering of light rays in the yellow-orange spectrum.

The phenotype in question has an orange forehead, throat, and upper breast. Its body is predominantly bright yellowish apple green, very similar to the Apple Green.

The Orangeface factor's effect is not confined to the face; the entire body is affected. It alters the entire phenotype and makes it possible to identify heterozygous birds definitely. The ground color of split (heterozygous) birds shows a bright orange cast. The green turns orangeish, the rectrices are strongly marked with a pinkish orange, and the periophthalmic feathers also receive an orange tinge. This is in fact an intermediate phenotype, comparable to a Medium Green, as is characteristic of incompletely dominant inheritance. The chicks' down is a bright orange, instead of being pale.

The Orangeface factor can be added to any ground color. If psittacin is present (yellow ground), we are going to have the orange-faced lovebirds; if not (non-yellow ground), the birds will have pale yellow faces. We think that the most beautiful combinations are made with Ino birds.

Yellowface. The results of combinations with other psittacin-diluting genes (Pastel and Whiteface) are not very beautiful, as there will be not enough carotenoid pigment to produce an attractive color. These birds are aptly called Yellowface by many fanciers. Being less attractive, such combinations have been avoided by many breeders, but this does not lessen their value, whether genetic or commercial. However, when the Dark factor is added, it very much enhances the bird's beauty: Yellowface Mauve, for example.

Orangeface Dark Green (Olive) *roseicollis.*

Orangeface Pastel *roseicollis.*

A heavily Pied Orangeface Medium Green (Jade) *roseicollis*.

Normal (wild coloration) A. *roseicollis.*

Cobalt Pastel (Medium Pastel) *roseicollis.*

Roseicollis **which are heterozygous for the Red-suffusion factor have rectrices which are almost totally melanic (black).**

THE RED-SUFFUSION FACTOR

This is one of the most controversial genes in agapornism. By many aviculturists and technicians it is not considered to be a chromosomal mutation. It alters pigment synthesis in the course of metabolism, though the biochemistry of this is not well defined. It appears to be inherited as an autosomal recessive. The expressivity and penetration of this gene are incomplete, which may be due to unidentified epistatic genes.

The carriers of this factor show a totally pink-rose color, a sort of flesh tone. It generally appears

Birds "split" for the Orangeface factor can be easily identified by the orange marks in the tail feathers (on left), instead of the rose pink of normal birds. In fact, the term *split* should be avoided, because the whole body is slightly orangeish, a characteristic of the third phenotype produced by an incompletely dominant character.

Red suffused Medium Green. Dark-factored Red-suffused birds are a beautiful dark bloody rose color.

Whiteface Dark Pastel (Mauve) *roseicollis*.

with the first molt; thus the birds are born green and with the first molt change into a fully red-suffused bird.

Red-suffused birds are quite rare, and seem to have a decreased longevity, compared to common birds; this may be a deleterious pleiotropism. We opine that there may be an accumulation of psittacofulvin in the barbs, as a result of overproduction or underdegradation. The real mechanisms involved are still unknown to us.

Normal and Red-suffusion heterozygote *roseicollis*. The melanic (black) rectrices of the bird on the left differ from the rose-pink-and-black coloration of the normal *roseicollis* form (right). This characteristic occurs in birds heterozygous for the Red-suffusion factor; this makes it easy to identify heterozygotes.

THE DANISH RED FACTOR

This bird appeared in 1990 in Denmark and then disappeared the following year. It may have been the first example of true erythrism in *Agapornis*, as it was a totally red bird with red eyes. It was born from a pair of Lutino

Danish Violet Apple Green American Cinnamon *roseicollis*.

Peach-face Lovebirds. Unhappily, this bird died before a bloodline could be started. Let's hope that this marvelous mutation will appear again somewhere.

THE GRAY PASTEL FACTOR

This strange and unpopular mutation appeared in 1986/87 in the aviaries of Mr. Bodo Ochs in Germany. Mr. Ochs didn't keep this bloodline. He sold two birds to Mr. Oliveira, who has been keeping them and increasing the population. Today it is quite well established in Brazil but is still rare.

A dominant mutation, it produces a phenotype intermediate between a Pastel and an Apple Green, just a bit paler and grayish, mainly in the ear coverts and primaries. This is not a good factor for combinations, as it is mainly visible on a Pastel ground color. It is a structural factor, and close observation reveals pigmentation deficits in the mantle, back, and wing coverts, resembling a very fine lace in a silk screen. At first glance, it can be mistaken for a Pastel.

THE GRAY FACTOR

This is probably the newest *roseicollis* mutation. It too appeared in Denmark toward the end of 1990 in Mr. Kloosterman's aviaries. He didn't have sufficient time and space to breed a stock of this mutation, and after a few crossings just two birds remained. These two birds nowadays are in good

Danish Redino *roseicollis*. This is certainly the first example of psittacofulvin schizochroic mutation in *Agapornis*. Photo by Mr. Johan Kloosterman.

Danish Redino *roseicollis*. This is certainly the first example of psittacofulvin schizochroic mutation in *Agapornis*. Photo by Mr. Johan Kloosterman.

health in the author's aviaries and are starting to breed.

So far, Gray in *roseicollis* has shown itself to be an autosomal recessive factor; however, other genetic mechanisms may be involved and may be disturbing the analysis.

These birds resemble a Medium Green but have a gray body shade overall and a bluish gray rump. The rachis is also gray. Split (heterozygous) birds are also similar to Medium Greens. Though I am not sure yet, this is probably an instance of true gray schizochroism, comparable to that found in Budgerigars and ring-necked parakeets.

Hybrid of Green *personata* and Lutino *roseicollis*. These birds are infertile. Such pairings should be avoided.

***Agapornis personata* and its mutations:**

MASKED LOVEBIRD MUTATIONS

One of the most popular lovebirds, the Masked Lovebird, *Agapornis personata personata,* in its wild color pattern is predominantly green, with breast, throat, and nape yellow. Black on the head suggests a hood, and it has a red beak and dark cinnamon irises.

The mutations of *personata* as a group are among the most beautiful in agapornism. So far there have been seven mutations, all of which follow defined genetic patterns.

THE BLUE FACTOR

The *personata* Blue mutation was the first to be reported in *Agapornis*. Its source seems to be a wild blue bird captured in Tanganyika and exported to the UK in a flock of normal-phenotype birds .

The blue color here is an optical effect known as *interference*. It is secondary to light dispersion in the median (cloudy) zone of the feathers when there is total absence of carotenoids (psittacin). What we have here is a true blue. In

Blue	*A*	*a*	AR	org
Dilute	*D*	*d*	AR	
Ino	*I*	*i*	AR-intlil, fisc	
Dark	*e*	*E*	AC	fisc-org
Fallow	*F*	*f*	AR	org.
Cinnamon	*C*	*c*	SLR	
Pied	*P*	*p*	AD	

Dilute Cobalt *personata.* The dilute factor (homozygous) combined with one Dark factor in a Blue bird makes a beautiful lilac color pattern.

Blue *personata*.

Agapornis truly blue mutations can be found only in *A. p. personata, A. p. fischeri,* and *A. p. nigrigenis.*

So far, its inheritance has been shown to follow the Mendelian autosomal recessive pattern. It is represented as *a*.

A large number of combinations can be made, the most common being the Dilute Blue, also erroneously known as White.

THE DILUTE FACTOR

The Dilute acts by decreasing the eumelanin concentration over the entire body, lightening every phenotype to which it is added (excepting the Ino-factor homozygote). An autosomal recessive, represented as *d*, it is responsible for several different phenotypes.

Dilute Green—Also called Yellow, this is a lemon yellow bird, with a greenish tone on the back and breast. The males tend to be lighter mainly on the back. The head must have a mask, or hood, like the wild phenotype but changed to a brownish hue. The iris is black, and the rachis is gray.

This combination, as the name suggests, adds the Dilute factor to the wild phenotype; i.e., a non-Blue, non-Ino bird (*IIAAdd*; see Example 6).

Bright Yellow—This is merely a Dilute Green with the addition of one Ino factor (heterozygous, or split, for Ino). The Ino factor, though recessive, potentiates the diluting action, and it produces a bird with a brighter, purer yellow color, free of green tones.

Mosaic Dilute Blue and a Green *personata*. This is an example of a somatic mutation. Eventually, such birds can transmit this coloration to their descendants, as they are also mosaics genotypically. The inheritance of this condition is complex, not simply Mendelian. In theory, breeding with rigorous selection will produce a thoroughly mutant strain of such birds.

Albino *personata*. This bird has completely white feathers and red eyes.

The brownish mask almost disappears completely.

Dilute Blue—Erroneously called White, this is a sky blue bird with a grayish mask, black iris, and a whitish back. The white suffusion on the back is more pronounced in males. This combination has the genotype *aadd*; see Example 6.

White—Just as the carotenoids (psittacin) are affected in non-Blue birds, the Dilute Blue is potentiated by the heterozygous Ino factor (*Iiaadd*). The result is an almost totally white bird, in many cases identical to an Albino except for the black eyes. This combination appears in Example 7.

THE INO FACTOR

Some of the most beautiful birds in agapornism are the result of the Ino factor: the Lutino *personata* and also the Albino.

Its origin is controversial. It seems that the mutation did not originate in *personata*. It may have been borrowed from *A. p. lilianae* or even from *A. p. fischeri* and selected over time.

The great similarity among the Ino forms in *personata, lilianae* and *fischeri* is, without doubt, greatly responsible for the large number of hybrids which have been spread throughout aviculture. This hybridization is often due to inexperience of aviculturists, who were not conscious of the importance of keeping these forms (whether viewed as species or as subspecies) pure.

Lutino *personata*.

Dark Green (Olive) *personata*.

The Ino factor operates as it does in *roseicollis* and provides the total absence of melanins, and consequently red eyes. Its inheritance is autosomal recessive and not sex-linked as in *roseicollis*. It is represented as *i*. Basically there are two resultant phenotypes:

Lutino—This is a magnificent bird of a bright golden yellow, quite uniform and almost luminescent. It has red eyes, crimson beak, salmon feet, and the forehead has a light orange suffusion.

Lutino will be visible only when the Ino factor is homozygous and the bird is non-Blue. It is epistatic to all other *personata* mutations, which means that further combinations such as Dilute Lutino, Dark (Olive) Lutino, Medium Dark Lutino, etc., are not visibly different.

Albino—The combination of the Blue and the Ino factors generates a totally non-melanin and non-psittacin bird. It is a bird with no pigments of any kind and so is totally snow white with red eyes: a true albino.

THE DARK FACTOR

Here, as in *roseicollis*, the Dark factor acts as a modifier of the phenotypes to which it is added. It alters structurally the median (cloudy) zone and increases the absorption of light rays, darkening the phenotype.

In *personata* the Dark gene is autosomal, codominant or

Fallow Green *personata*. The red eyes and dilute green body color are characteristic of this rare, beautiful mutation.

Dilute Green *personata*, poorly marked. The head is brownish and the throat tinged with orange, which are characteristics of hybrids of *personata* and *fischeri.*

incompletely dominant. So far we have not detected in *personata* the phenotypic variability we find with the *roseicollis* Dark factor, so for the present we will treat it as a single gene that can give us the following phenotypes.

Medium Green, or Jade— Similar to the wild phenotype but darker and brighter. The black is stronger, and the upper tail coverts are foggy lilac. This is just a normal Green bird heterozygous for the Dark factor (*Ee*).

Dilute Medium Green—This phenotype results from adding a single Dark factor to a Dilute Green bird (*EeA-dd*). Compared to a normal Dilute Green, the green is considerably darker, the yellow exhibits an ocher suffusion, and the mask is brown.

Medium Blue, or Cobalt— Exceptional beauty is characteristic of the Cobalt *personata*, which the result of adding one Dark factor to a Blue bird (*EeaaD-*). The name Cobalt closely corresponds to its actual color. The black mask is quite a bit darker and contrasts with the white collar. Some Cobalt birds have a quite violaceous cast; this may be a sign of an intrinsic factor interacting with the Dark inheritance. Or it may be a sign of pureness, as we have observed that strains that carry *fischeri* blood are lighter and less metallic in the color suffusion.

Dilute Medium Blue—This is

Poorly marked *personata*. The ill-defined mask is brownish, instead of pure black; an orange suffusion appears on the yellow upper breast. This bird is split for Ino, being the result of a test mating between a supposedly pure normal and a supposedly pure Lutino. Its appearance suggests that the Lutino parent has *fischeri* blood. Some dilution can occur even with pure Lutino birds, but not to this extent.

a lilac, sky blue bird, somewhat purplish. It can be obtained by the addition of one Dark factor to a Dilute Blue bird (*Eeaadd*).

Dark Green, or Olive—An olivaceous green bird, with an ocher yellow breast; the black mask is sometimes tinged with ocher. It results from the presence of two Dark (homozygote) factors in a Green bird (EEA-D-).

Dilute Dark Green—This is a Dark Green bird plus two Dilute factors (*EEA-dd*). It is a yellowish ocher bird, sometimes very close to a cinnamon color.

Dark Blue, or Slate, or Mauve—A Blue bird with no carotenoid (psittacin) pigments and homozygous Dark factors (*EEaaD-*), its coloration is generally slate, with a white collar and a black mask.

Dilute Dark Blue—The addition of Dilute factors to the bird just mentioned produces a light, ashy gray white-collared bird with a gray mask (*EEaadd*). Two phenotypes have been observed, one lighter and one darker. This may be a first sign of the existence of Dark complex in *personata*; yet we must be cautious in our analysis, as it may just be an expression of distant *fischeri* genes.

THE FALLOW FACTOR

One of the more recent mutations in agapornism, it appeared about 1986-87 in the USA, and there are still very few fully colored birds.

The Fallow, or Fawn, factor is inherited as an autosomal recessive; it is represented as *f*. It effects the absence of eumelanin (black melanin), giving us a brownish green bird with a brownish gray mask. In the future we will certainly get very good Fallow combinations.

Unhappily, as yet we have little trustworthy data on Fallow *personata*, but it seems likely that the females are problematical: their eggs may be soft, as happens with the Japanese Yellow *roseicollis* hens.

THE CINNAMON FACTOR

From several locations around the world, reports have been heard about the occurrence of a Cinnamon factor in *personata*, mainly in Australia. The literature tells us that its inheritance is sex-linked. However, the author himself has so far never seen such birds.

THE PIED FACTOR

This is another controversial topic. The existance of this factor has been announced sporadically around the world, and very beautiful birds have even been shown. Unfortunately, these have been proved to be modifications, and not the result of true mutations. Recently we have learned that in Australia there is a true Pied mutation, and that a strain is being developed.

Fallow Green *personata* (Masked Lovebird). The red eyes together with a dilute green body color is characteristic of this rare beautiful mutation.

Dilute Dark Blue (Dilute Mauve) *personata*.

Dilute Blue *personata*.

Dark Blue (Mauve) *personata*. Here you can see that two Dark factors are able to change a true blue color into a gray color.

Dilute Medium Green *personata*. This is a double Dilute, single Dark-factored Green bird.

Green *personata* (Wild pattern). Pure birds must have no orange suffusion on the throat. The yellow collar takes all neck perimeter.

Green *personata* (Wild pattern). Pure birds must have no orange suffusion on the throat. The yellow collar takes all neck perimeter.

***Agapornis personata lilianae* and its mutations:**

NYASA LOVEBIRD MUTATIONS

Throughout the world *A. p. lilianae*, the Nyasa Lovebird, is considered a rarity. Aviculturally, this bird is mainly found in the Americas, and it also seems to be relatively common in Australia. A little smaller than the other *personata* subspecies, this form has a greenish yellow head with an orange face. There are certainly two mutations that originated in *lilianae*, both in Australia. Also, both are autosomal recessives.

THE INO FACTOR

The *lilianae* Ino factor is one of the oldest mutations in agapornism, first appearing in 1936 in Mr. A. Prendergast's aviaries in Adelaide, Australia. It may be the source of all the Ino factors found in other *personata* forms; that is, "borrowed" by means of hybridization. All we know is that pure Lutino *lilianae* are extremely rare outside of Australia; even non-pures are quite rare. Inherited as an autosomal recessive, the Ino factor is represented as *i*, while the non-Ino, or normal, gene is *I*.

This extremely beautiful lovebird is a golden yellow, with red eyes, white primary vane and rachis, salmon feet, and the face and throat are a bright reddish orange. The beak is crimson with a pearl base.

Agapornis personata lilianae.

THE DILUTE FACTOR

This is one of the rarest mutations, unknown to many people. Its origin is uncertain. A pair of Dilute *lilianae* were offered by a local dealer called Brush in Ausburn City, Australia. Since that occasion, they've become more widespread, but outside Australia there are not many pure specimens. Its inheritance is autosomal recessive, like other dilute genes in the *personata* group (Dilute *d*, non-Dilute *D*).

An enormous number of Dilute *lilianae* are offered as pure, but unfortunately they are nothing but hybrid birds, which have been produced mainly in Europe.

OTHER MUTATIONS

In late 1994,I was notified by Mr. Enrique Santos about Blue *lilianae* in Portugal. Unfortunately, I have not been able to ascertain the circumstances of its origin; it may be wild caught.

Several crossings of *lilianae* and *fischeri* have been made and some Dark-factor birds produced. Again, I shall counsel breeders to avoid such techniques and procedures.

Lutino *lilianae*. Note the reddish orange covering the entire head and upper breast to the upper abdomen. This is the coloration of a pure Lutino *lilianae*.

Lilianae. Pure birds have a bright orange front that contrasts with a deep green. There is a slightly yellowish band on the nape.

***Agapornis personata nigrigenis* and its mutations:**

BLACK-CHEEKED LOVEBIRD MUTATIONS

The Black-cheeked Lovebirds, *A. p. nigrigenis*, are the smallest birds in the genus and are among the most highly evolved. They are rare, but not more so than *lilianae*. There are only two original mutations, the Blue factor and the Yellow factor.

THE BLUE FACTOR

It first appeared in Denmark, where it has been propagated regularly, though it has not become widespread. An autosomal recessive, it is represented as *a*, while the normal allele is *A*.

The author has traveled all over Europe and seen several Blue *nigrigenis*, but only the Danish Blue can be safely considered to be a pure mutation! The others are all selected from crossings among *nigrigenis* and Blue *personata*. The hybrids are bigger, have a misproportioned head that lacks the characteristic pearl mark at the base of the beak. It can be difficult to distinguish such a bird from a poor Blue *personata*.

THE YELLOW FACTOR

This mutation—perhaps the newest among lovebirds—appeared in Denmark in 1991-92 in a flock of wild-colored birds. At present, unfortunately, only split birds remain, as all the Yellow birds died early in 1993.

This variety is a very beautiful greenish golden yellow. The black in the cheeks becomes a pale brownish orange. The beak is orange, preserving the pearl at its base.

Of autosomal recessive inheritance, the Yellow factor is represented as *y*, and its normal allele is *Y*. This new mutation makes the White, or Yellow-and-Blue, combination possible in *nigrigenis*.

OTHERS MUTATIONS

Other *nigrigenis* mutations—such as Dilute and Dark—without doubt originated from hybridization with *personata* and *fischeri* and then further selection through considered pairings. These procedures should be avoided, but Dilute and Dark-factor *nigrigenis* can be found.

We hope that in the future we will hear of other new mutations that are pure *nigrigenis*. An Ino *nigrigenis* has been reported recently; described as an autosomal recessive, I have doubts about its origin and pureness.

Yellow *nigrigenis*. That the areas of color conform to that of the wild form is an indication of pureness. Photo by Johan Kloosterman.

Blue *nigrigenis*. The bright white spot on the throat surrounded by a blackish gray is characteristic of a pure Blue *nigrigenis*.

***Agapornis personata fischeri* and its mutations:**

FISCHER'S LOVEBIRD MUTATIONS

Fischer's Lovebird, *A. p. fischeri*, is quite common in world of aviculture, with the exception of South America, where pure birds are becoming increasingly rarer, particularly the wild phenotype, which is less frequently seen than the Dilute Green.

The *fischeri* mutations are basically the same as those found in *Agapornis personata personata*, but with some exceptions.

THE DILUTE FACTOR

The *fischeri* Dilute factor, like the *personata* Dilute, decreases the black melanin (eumelanin) concentration, thereby lightening the phenotype. The result is a clear greenish yellow or a clear sky blue, depending on the presence or absence of psittacin (carotenoids). Its inheritance is autosomal recessive. The following phenotypes appear:

Dilute Green—may be the most common Fischer's mutation. However, due to its similarity to the *personata* Dilute Green, the two forms have been hybridized by less experienced aviculturists. Pure Dilute *fischeri* are rare, and we must always attempt to avoid non-pure birds.

Dilute Blue—The combination of the Dilute and the Blue factors results a sky blue bird, with breast and forehead white, and having a light grayish crown and nape. We can obtain Dilute Blue

FISCHER'S LOVEBIRD, *A.P. FISCHERI*

Factor	*Normal Allele*	*Mutant Allele*	*Mode of Inheritance*
Dilute	*D*	*d*	AR
Yellow	*Y*	*y*	AR
Blue	*A*	*a*	AR
Ino	*I*	*i*	AR
Golden	*g*	*G*	AD
Pied	*P*	*p*	*AR*
Dark	*e*	*E*	AC
Lime	*G2*	*g2*	AR
Featherfooted	*s*	*S*	AC
Greenwing	*W*	*w*	AR
Fallow	*F*	*f*	AR
Violet	*v*	*V*	AD

by following the example on page 54.

THE YELLOW FACTOR

This almost unknown factor originated in Australia, but all the birds were exported to South Africa, where they have stayed so far. There are recent records of the arrival of some of these birds in Belgium, but the author, during recent travels in Europe, was able to trace them only to Portugal.

This is a true Yellow factor, with an almost complete absence of melanin, except for the eyes, which are black. It is a totally golden yellow bird, identical in color tone to the Lutino, but in addition to the black eyes it has also gray legs. Combined with the Blue, a totally snow white, black-eyed bird results.

We can even hypothesize that it could be an allele of the Ino factor, construing it as a partial lutinism similar to that of the Ino factor in *roseicollis*. It is said to be an autosomal recessive factor (represented as *y*), but we need to propagate this mutation further and become better acquainted with the manner in which it is inherited.

THE BLUE FACTOR

The *fischeri* Blue mutation seems to have originated in that part of Europe which was called Czechoslovakia. A few birds of this pure strain were dispersed through Europe. Unfortunately, there are several *personata*-hybrid strains throughout the world, so the great majority of

Blue *fischeri*. Pure birds must exhibit a pure white.

Blue *fischeri* are derived from them. Another pure Blue line is found in the USA, where it appeared about 1981 or 1982. An autosomal recessive, it is represented as *a*.

THE INO FACTOR

In expression the *fischeri* Lutino (non-Blue) and Albino (Blue) birds are like the Inos in *personata*. Homozygotic birds are totally non-melanic, while the heterozygotes will show intermediate phenotypes: bright yellow (Dilute Green/Ino) and light white (Dilute Blue/Ino). As in *lilianae*, its likely source, in *fischeri* too, inheritance is autosomal recessive; the factor is representeed as *i*.

THE DARK FACTOR

This mutation, which affects structural colors, also appears to have been "borrowed" from *personata*, and its inheritance is the same. In *fischeri*, the Dark factor has a different expressivity: it does not darken the phenotypes as much as in *personata*; the Dark *fischeri* are considerably lighter. Thus it can be used to assess evidence of hybridization, as pure *personata* are quite dark when they carry the Dark factor.

THE GOLDEN FACTOR

This recent, quite beautiful mutation may have first appeared in Switzerland. It is a diluting factor, autosomal dominant (represented as *G*), and specimems are sexually dimorphic. They are a bright marbled yellow, similar to the pattern found on the wing coverts of American Yellow *roseicollis*. Male birds are more greenish on the back and are easily distinguished from the females, which are quite yellow and bright.

Blue *fischeri*. The characteristic markings of this form are preserved in the Blue mutation.

Penetrance of the autosomal-dominant Golden factor is incomplete, however, which means that only a small percentage of mutant birds will result from a pairing with a normal bird. Yet these birds are quite robust, and probably soon we shall see an increase in their numbers throughout the world. More males are born than females, and this may sometimes be a problem.

Dark Green Olive *fischeri.*

Dilute Medium Green Double Golden *fischeri.* The Dark factor makes beautifully contrasting colors and markings evident.

Dilute Silver *fischeri.* In *fischeri*, Silver is the Blue form of the Golden factor.

Sable *fischeri*. Photo courtesy of *Australian Birdkeeper Magazine* and Mr. Roy Havesi.

Medium Blue (Cobalt) *fischeri.*

Dilute Medium Green (Jade) *fischeri*.

Dark Blue (Mauve) *fischeri*.

THE LIME FACTOR

As with all new mutations originating in Australia, we do not have much data about this one. It is very similar to the Golden factor, but with an autosomal-recessive inheritance; therefore it is represented as *g2*. It seems that Limes have been bred regularly in Australia in the last year, but due to various restrictions and the bureaucracy in Australia, we have no records of this mutation outside that country. As this mutation appears similar to the *fischeri* Dilute factor, we may wonder whether it is the same gene, or an allele of it.

THE PIED FACTOR

I have seen some beautiful Pied *fischeri*, quite well marked. Unfortunately, so far, none have been proved to be true chromosomal mutations, just modifications. Golden *fischeri* can eventually produce pied birds.

True Pied birds may have appeared last year in Portugal in the aviaries of Mr. Enrique Santos. Bred from wild-caught stock, some of these have already gone on to breed. There may be a difference in expressivity between single- and double-factored birds, as the latter are more heavily pied.

THE FEATHERFOOTED FACTOR

This very interesting mutation does not affect the birds' coloration. It merely causes feathers to grow on their feet. Heavily feathered birds do occur, but some are only slightly feathered on their feet. This may

Yellow *fischeri*. A white-rumped bird with black eyes, this variety has no connection with the Ino factor.

Blue and Green *fischeri*. Photo courtesy of *Australian Birdkeeper Magazine* and Mr. Roy Havesi.

Medium Green (Jade) *fischeri*. Photo by Mr. Bernd Ziegenfuss.

be related to homo- or heterozygosis, which suggests that this is a codominant mutation; but further studies must be done.

THE GREENWING FACTOR

Perhaps the most recent true mutation in *Agapornis*, it is being established in Portugal, where it may have originated from wild-caught birds.

The name of this mutation points out the fact that this yellow bird, with the orange forehead and paler breast than in the normal *fischeri*, has green wings. As yet, the inheritance of this mutation is not well understood, but it appears to be an autosomal recessive (represented as *w*). Perhaps it is a kind of dilute factor. Its interaction with the various other extant mutations has not yet been investigated.

Sable *fischeri*, juvenile. Note the black striping on the beak; this phenomenon is unique to Blue *fischeri* juveniles. Photo courtesy of *Australian Birdkeeper Magazine* and Mr. Roy Havesi.

Cobalt (left) and Blue *fischeri*. Photo by Mr. Bernd Ziegenfuss.

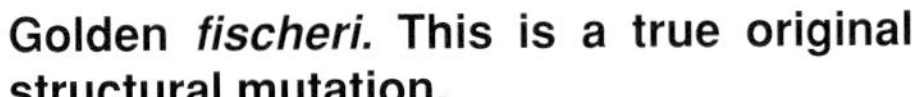

Golden *fischeri.* This is a true original structural mutation.

Green (wild type) *fischeri.*

THE FALLOW FACTOR

Yet another mutation in agapornism originated in Australia. Known there as the Avocado, it appeared about 1992 and has been established by Mr. Roy Hevesi. So far, this factor appears to exhibit autosomal-recessive inheritance, and is represented as *f*.

This is a dilute green bird with a buff yellow mantle and purplish eyes (chicks have very light pink to plum eyes). Adults look like "Opal" birds; perhaps this would be more accurate than Fallow. Mr. Hevesi has given the name Sable to the the Avocado-and-Blue combination. In adult birds the iris darkens. The chicks do show black striping on the beak, even in Blue varieties; this phenomenon has not occurred in other dilute mutations so far.

White *fischeri.* Completely white, with black eyes, without involving the Ino factor.

Dilute Double Golden *fischeri*. In this variety, the orange on the head is enhanced.

Greenwing *fischeri*, one of the newest mutations. Photo by Mr. Enrique Santos.

Dilute Green *fischeri*. A pure orange color on the forehead is required in true Dilute *fischeri*.

THE VIOLET FACTOR

The newest lovebird mutation and its inheritance is autosomal dominant and similar to the *roseicollis* violet factor. The author thinks that further crossings must be done to get to know the entire genetic mechanisms and their actual interactions with other fischers' factors. If it really is similar to *roseicollis*, the entire set of genetic combinations can also be achieved with fischer series.

Hybridization in *Personatas*

HYBRIDIZATION IN LOVEBIRDS

The lovebirds of the *personata* group (*personata, fischeri, lilianae* and *nigrigenis*), commonly known as the "eye-ringed group," are very closely related genetically. Matings among any of these forms will produce fertile hybrids.

Many of the mutations in this group, particularly the homozygotic Dilutes, are phenotypically extremely similar. Because the forms can be so easily confused, less experienced aviculturists will pair their birds erroneously. Pairing *personata* mutations with those of *fischeri* is a common mistake. Such matings are a fact, and, unhappily, they are tending to become more frequent in agapornism, due to the lack of information and the pressures of the market.

The Ino factor is especially susceptible to uncontrolled hybridization, as the Lutino forms of *lilianae, personata* and *fischeri* are extremely similar, although distinguishable by trained eyes.

Unfortunately, hybridization is used by many breeders as a common method of gene transference. It seems to us that the *personata* group's Ino factor comes exclusively from *lilianae* (although there is a possibility that a *fischeri* Ino mutation originated in the USA). That the Ino occurs in other forms as a "borrowed" factor is really unfortunate. Nowadays it is extremely rare to find pure eye-ringed Lutinos anywhere in the world except Australia. It seems that the Dark factor—and even the Blue factor—is going to be spread in the same uncontrolled way.

Pureness must be the aim of people involved in agapornism, or any other part of aviculture. Hybridization must be avoided in every way, except when undertaken in highly controlled scientific experiments.

Identification Key to *personata* Mutations:

DILUTE FACTOR (Green, not blue)

Head

lilianae: Reddish orange mask delimited in the throat and auriculars.

personata: Grayish brown mask involving crown and nape borders as well.

fischeri: Orange forehead and throat; crown and nape foggy olive yellow.

nigrigenis: Facial mask gray, tinged with brown in the borders, throat, and auriculars.

Neck

lilianae: Dull yellow.

personata: Yellow.

fischeri: Lemon yellow.

nigrigenis: Olive yellow.

Breast

lilianae: Yellowish green.

personata: Greenish yellow.

Golden *Agapornis p. fischeri*. This is true structural original mutation.

fischeri: Lemon yellow.

nigrigenis: Olive yellow.

(Here we have hypothesized that there is a true original mutation in the *nigrigenis* form.)

To describe, and to distinguish, the details in birds of the Dilute-and-Blue combination is a little bit more difficult. The outlines of the colored areas that characterize each form is preserved, but white/gray shades are substituted for the corresponding yellow/orange colors.

INO FACTOR

Head

lilianae: Intense orange red forehead, throat, and upper breast.

personata: Yellow, slightly tinged with orange in auriculars.

fischeri: Intense orange forehead and throat.

Beak

lilianae: Bright red with ivory base.

personata: Bright crimson.

fischeri: Orange red.

The remainder of the body is gold yellow with white primaries.

Albinos (the combination of Ino and Blue) in *personata* and *fischeri* are totally indistinguishable in appearance.

(Note that it is premature to include the *nigrigenis* Ino and *lilianae* Blue factors.)

Hybrids of these forms, whether Dilute or Ino, exhibit intermediate patterns in coloration, with poorly defined facial masks, and also intermediate head and beak shapes!

Whitefaced American Cinnamon *roseicollis.*

OTHER LOVEBIRD SPECIES

Agapornis cana, the Grey-headed or Madagascar Lovebird, belongs to the most primitive evolutionary group in the genus *Agapornis*. Sexual dimorphism is pronounced: the male has a bluish white head and breast but the female is totally green. These lovebirds are quite aggressive. They reproduce regularly in captivity, yet they are still rare, found mainly in the Americas.

***A. cana* female.**

Breeding in colonies should be avoided due to their aggressiveness. A nest box furnished with a short tube at the entrance is advisable, because they are very shy. The behavior and care of *cana* have already been described in Chapters 2 and 3.

Recently announced is the appearance of the first *cana* mutation: a Lutino cock in the USA. Its inheritance pattern seems still to be uncertain, though it may be an autosomal recessive. We hope that this and other *cana* mutations may spread worldwide.

Agapornis pullaria, known as the Red-faced or San Tome Island Lovebird is unique in agapornism. This species is quite rare. Sexual dimorphism is distinct but not pronounced: males forehead, throat, and beak are bright orange red; females are duller and reddish orange instead of orange red.

A. cana male.

A. cana male.

Green predominates, and the primaries are black.

Its peculiar nesting behavior is the main cause of the low number of *pullaria* in captivity (see Chapters 2 and 3). Of the two mutations, both occurred in the wild, and the birds were brought into captivity. These are very rare and may disappear. The Blue factor, *a*, is an autosomal, recessive to the noraml gene, *A*. The Ino is also autosomal, *i* being recessive to the normal *I*.

Agapornis taranta, the Abyssinian Lovebird, is the largest member of the genus. It is sexually dimorphic and breeds quite regularly in captivity but is still rare. The males are green with the forehead and beak bright red; females are totally green with a red beak.

Several reports on *taranta* mutations have emerged over the years, but little is known about their status and modes of inheritance. There are fawn and gray schizochroics, and cinnamon, blue, and dark mutations, and it's likely that these factors behave genetically in a fashion similar to their counterparts in other lovebird species.

Agapornis swinderniana, the Black-collared Lovebird, is one of the rarest bird species, and certainly the most unfamiliar lovebird. All attempts to keep them in captivity have failed. Also, very little is known about their habits and behavior in the wild, and so far there have been no reports of mutations observed there.

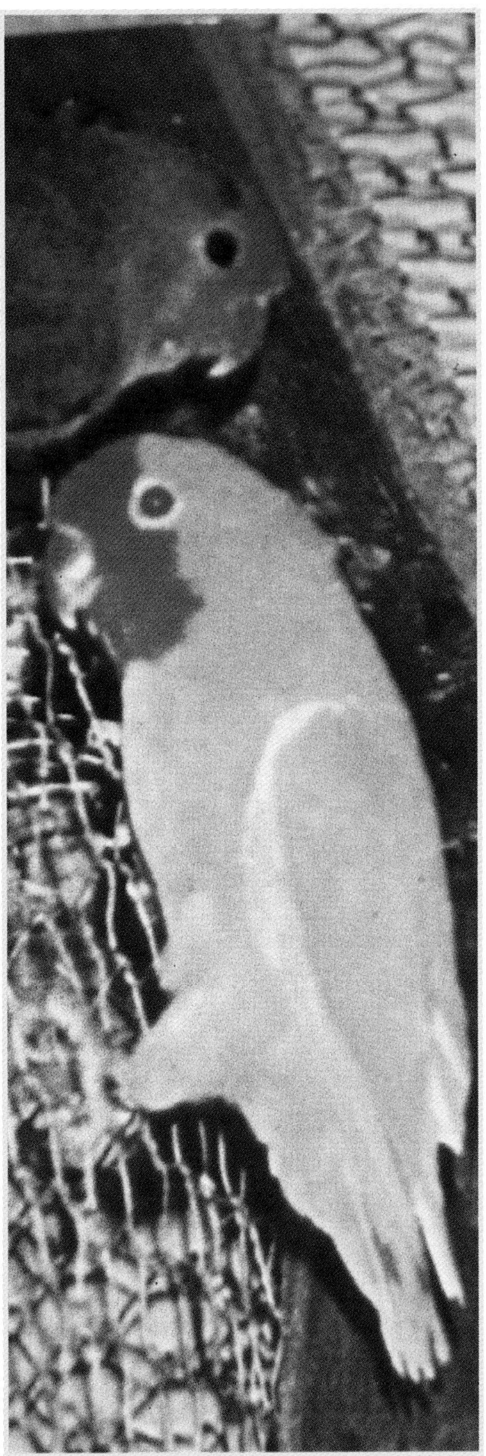

Lutino *pullaria*. Photo by A.S.B. Coelho. Taken from *The Book of Lovebirds and Related Parrots* by George A. Smith. Paul Elek Ltd. London 1979.

Pair of *Agapornis pullaria.* Females have a less intense red face. Photo by Mr. Johan Kloosterman.

***A. taranta* pair.**

A. taranta female.

A. taranta male.

A.swinderniana swinderniana **(left)**
A.swinderniana zenkeri **(right).**
Drawn by Mrs. Rosana D'Angieri.

AGAPORNIS DISEASES

Lovebirds are extremely strong and healthy birds, but, like all living beings, they are susceptible to parasites and pathogenic microorganisms. Some are common to birds in general, some specific to the Psittacidae, and others specific to the genus *Agapornis.*

The great majority of the diseases they are susceptible to are cosmopolitan. Yet, some diseases are endemic in certain countries, which makes it prudent to quarantine any new bird in your aviaries.

Differential diagnosis is not always possible; indeed, it may present difficulties most of the time, especially with viral diseases, for which laboratory methods for clinical analysis are not available everywhere. Often diagnoses are possible only postmortem. In some instances, even with a diagnosis in hand, no effective treatment exists.

We must keep in mind some basic principles in order to achieve success in avian treatment: At the first suspicion of sickness, the bird must be isolated, diagnoses must be done as soon as possible, and treatment promptly set. Remember that the smaller the species, the more quickly the practitioner needs to proceed with the therapy.

The sick bird must be kept warm. The environmental temperature must be increased to 85°F. The bird's diet must be supplemented with vitamins and amino acids. Injectable multivitamins can be used.

We do not intend this chapter as a survey of avian medicine, but we are going to try to provide a concise review of the diseases that mainly affect the *agapornis,* making it possible for the aviculturist to identify and initiate therapy for the principal ones.

BACTERIAL INFECTIONS

There is an uncountable number of bacteria that can produce the most various kinds of infections, from localized to septicemic ones. Many clinical signs can be present; in general we have:

External infections: Erythema and edema may be present in lacerations and external wounds. Deeper wounds can cause abscesses.

Paralysis of the extremities (legs or wings) can be a sign of injury or infectious arthritis-synovitis, for which the most common agents are *Streptococcus* and *Staphylococcus.*

Normally spontaneous cure is obtained, but it may be necessary to use antibiotics and even surgery. Septicemia can occur in some infections, such as pneumonias.

The treatment is based on antibiotic therapy. As often as possible, identification of the pathogen must be done by

Agapornis personata nigrigenis. Wild coloration. A small head and beak are characteristic of pureness. This is a very healthy bird.

culturing, and an appropriate antibiotic applied. A simple Gram's stain can assist in a differential diagnosis.

Gastrointestinal infections: One of the most common group of diseases; it can be the clinical expression of a systemic disease. There are also bacteria that directly affect the intestines, causing diarrhea, dehydration, septicemia, and death.

The main point in the treatment of diarrhea is to keep the bird well hydrated and warm. This can be accomplished using oral rehydraters and/or intravenous Ringers's solution.

The clinical signs of dehydration are: dry skin, dry mucosa, increased heart rate, lethargy and shock resulting in death.

A direct treatment countering the enteropathogenic agent may be necessary, after its identification by Gram's stain and a fecal culture.

The most common enteric agents are: *Escherichia coli*, *Salmonella* sp., *Citrobacter* sp., *Klebsiella* sp., *Pasteurella* sp., *Haemophilus* sp., *Campylobacter* sp., and *Pseudomonas* sp.

A variety of antibiotics are widely used. We should always be certain to do antimicrobial susceptibility testing before making a choice from those available. The following list contains those antibiotics most useful with lovebirds.

Principal Antibiotics Used with *Agapornis:*

Amikacin(1): 5 mg/kg, twice a day, I.M.

Amoxicillin(2): 50 mg/kg, orally every 8 hours.

Ampicillin(2): 50 mg/kg, orally every 8 hours.

Carbenicillin(1): 100 mg/kg twice a day, I.M. or I.V.

Cefotaxime(2): 50 mg/kg every 8 hours I.M.

Cephalexin(2): 10 mg/kg orally every 6 hours.

Cephalothin(2): 25 mg/kg every 6 hours, I.M.

Chloramphenicol(3): 15 mg/kg, orally every 6 hours.

Chlortetracycline(4): 10 mg/kg/ dose, orally every 6 hours or I.M.

Erythromycin(3): 20 mg/kg, orally every 12 hours.

Gentamicin(1): 3 mg/kg, every 8 hours I.M.

Lincomycin(2): 5 mg/kg, orally every 6 hours.

Tylosin(5): 15 mg/kg, every 8 hours I.M.

Trimethoprim(2): 8 mg/kg, orally every 12 hours.

Sulfamethoxazole(2): 20 mg/kg, orally every 12 hours.

(1) Acts on gram-negative agents.

(2) Acts mainly on gram-positives, may act on some gram-negative.

(3) Acts on gram-positive.

(4) Acts on gram-positive, gram-negative and anaerobics.

(5) For chronic upper respiratory diseases and/or initial therapy in acute ones.

Antifungals for use with *Agapornis*:

Ketoconazole: 5 mg/kg, orally every 12 hours for at least 12 days; it can be toxic.

Nystatin: 10,000 U dose, orally every 12 hours; it may cause diarrhea.

N.B.: A lovebird weighs about 40 g (0.04 kg.). To calculate the correct dose, just multiply the mg/kg dose by 0.04 to obtain the dose to be used.

Psittacosis—Ornithosis

Among the infectious diseases is one that deserves special attention, namely, ornithosis, also known as psittacosis, or chlamydiosis. It can infect any bird species, and occasionally human beings.

The agent is *Chlamydia psittaci*, an intercellular parasite, of worldwide distribution and endemic in those regions to which parrotlike birds are native. It is supposed that about 1% of the wild population carry *Chlamydia* in a natural equilibrium, with no signs or symptoms of disease. It seems that this disease manifests its pathology only in captive birds.

The chicks and youngsters are the most susceptible to the disease, and transmission is fecal-oral, mainly the aerogenic route. An acute systemic infection in youngsters is lethal most of the time, varying with the virulence and antigenicity of the chlamydial strain, but it can cause a completely asymptomatic infection in adult birds.

Incubation time varies with the bird species and chlamydial strain, ranging from 42 days to one year. The main symptoms are: sinusitis, dyspnea, conjunctivitis (often unilateral), dehydration, diarrhea and polyuria, hypothermia, lethargy, renal failure, shock, and death. The feces become yellowish due to hepatic failure. Subacute and chronic cases have been described. Central nervous system symptoms such as tonic-clonic movements, tremor, opisthotonus, and convulsions may appear. These can be the first signs to be observed, as the acute or subacute cases can be asymptomatic. Thyroid and adrenal damages may occur, leading to poor feathering and plumage. Secondary conjunctivitis is frequent. Sterility may occur in recovered birds.

Diagnosis is basically accomplished from the clinical signs and clinical history. Laboratory diagnoses using cell imprintings and smears may reveal Levinthal-Coles-Lillie bodies, which are pathognomonic of chlamydiosis. Differential diagnoses should be done with some viral diseases (herpesvirus, paramyxovirus, influenza) and enterobacteria.

Treatment is based on tetracyclines for 21 days.

FUNGAL INFECTIONS

Fungal infections, or mycotic diseases, generally occur in weak birds that are poorly kept, malnourished, and sick. Heavy exposure to fungi, in wet and shaded environments with high concentration of spores, increases the likelihood. Of the mycotic diseases, two are the most common: Aspergillosis and Candidiasis.

Aspergillosis

Aspergillus fumigatus is the etiological agent of aspergillosis, the most commonly seen opportunistic mycotic disease in immunosuppressed,

Oral candidiasis in a Peach-face Lovebird.

malnourished birds, as well as in birds subjected to protracted antibiotic treatment.

Aspergillosis mainly affects the respiratory tract, acutely and chronically; the trachea, syrinx, bronchi, and lungs, along with the air sacs, are affected. Granulomatous nodules (mycaetomas) are common in the chronic cases.

The clinical view is a lethargic bird, anorexic, with progressive loss of weight, voice change, dyspnea, and sudden death.

Diagnosis, which may be difficult, is done by fungi culture, serology, and biopsy of the nodules. It is not uncommon that diagnoses are made only postmortem.

Treatment is in fact not effective; the available drugs are in general toxic and prognosis is not good. Some of the drugs are:

Amphotericin B: 0.5 mg/kg, I.V. every 8 hours, for three days; 1.0 mg/kg intratracheal, once a day for three days; or 1.0 mg/ml solution to nebulize, twice a day.

5-fluorocytosina: 100 mg/kg, orally every 12 hours for 14 days.

Ketoconazole: 4–10 mg/kg, orally every 12 hours for 14 days.

Multivitamins and amino acids must be supplied during treatment.

Candidiasis

Birds with hypovitaminosis A, or those weak and stressed, are particularly susceptible to the fungus *Candida albicans*. It is commonly found at low levels in the digestive tract of all normal and healthy birds.

The disease progresses from the mouth to the crop and intestines. It usually causes crop impaction in baby *agapornis*, and systemic disease may occur. Malnutrition occurs secondarily from a deficient absorption of vitamins and other elements by the affected mucosa. A diphtheroid pseudomembrane is observed in the crop and often on the oral mucosa. A delayed emptying of the crop, which may be dilated, is also observed. Loss of weight, nausea, and regurgitation may also be seen.

Treatment is done with ketoconazole and nystatin (see antifungal table above).

VIRAL INFECTIONS

The virus genera that parasitize lovebirds and birds in general are extremely numerous. Since *Agapornis* is our main interest, we will focus on the following ones:

Poxvirus

With avipoxvirus, seventeen strains are known, all DNA formed. They produce intracytoplasmic, lipophilic inclusion bodies (Bölinger bodies) in the epithelium; such bodies are pathognomonic of avipoxvirosis.

Agapornis poxvirus is specific to lovebirds.

Transmission occurs both by vectors (mosquitoes) and environmental contamination, mainly in the summer. The virus is on the feathers, skin, and feces. It is spread by close contact of the birds and through traumatic lesions (the intact epithelium cannot be penetrated by avipoxvirus).

Gray Green *roseicollis.* This is the first record of Gray factor in *Agapornis.* There is a gray shade on the body's green; the rump is a grayish blue. New colors most often are not caused by communicable disease.

Whiteface Dark Pastel Cinnamon (Whiteface Cinnamon Mauve) roseicollis.

Two clinical stages are distinguished: (1) Inoculation—when it occurs, the virus propagates in the liver and bone marrow. (2) Viremia—when the virus is disseminated after its propagation.

Two main clinical forms are known: (1) The cutaneous form, which is the most common, consists of papules in the periophthalmic skin area, beak, and legs. Yellowish in the beginning, it darkens to a dark brown, desquamating spontaneously after some weeks and leaving no scars. Bacterial infections can occur secondarily. (2) The diphtheritic form is similar to the cutaneous form; it may coat the oral mucosa, tongue, pharynx, and larynx with a fibrous exudate and also is a grayish brown pseudomembrane that bleeds if it is removed. Obstruction of the trachea can also occur.

A third clinical form, the septicemic, has not been described for *Agapornis* poxvirus yet. The birds exhibit a ruffled plumage, dyspnea and somnolence, anorexia, and cyanosis. Death follows within hours. This form occurs mainly in immunosuppressed birds; it may occur without the cutaneous and diphtheroid forms.

Coryza can be commonly caused by pox virus, together with secondary bacterial infection and conjunctivitis. Pox virus is oncogenic and causes cutaneous tumors.

Diagnoses is obtained by fecal culture and biopsy, which reveal the pathognomonic Böllinger bodies. As there is no specific treatment, and we must take the following general measures:

-Isolate the sick birds in clean cages protected from mosquitoes.

-Offer multivitamins, mainly vitamins A and C, orally or intravenously.

-Antibiotics must be administered in case of bacterial infections.

-Keep the environment at about 90° F.

-Tincture of iodine can be applied to cutaneous lesions.

-Immunomodulators can be used, though their effectiveness is unproved.

Agapornis poxvirus is serologically specific, but we know of no available vaccine.

Herpesvirus—Pacheco's Disease

There are several herpesviruses, but here we are going to mention the one that is responsible for Pacheco's disease.

General symptoms are somnolence, lethargy, anorexia, ruffled plumage, and diarrhea. If the liver is involved, the feces become yellowish. Secondary infections are frequent, mainly pneumonia causing dyspnea. Intestinal bleeding and convulsions may occur.

Virus is eliminated in the feces, the main contamination route. Hygienic practices are essential to control epidemics, and diagnosis is accomplished by visualization of herpesvirus inclusion bodies. There is no specific treatment.

Paramyxovirus (PMV)

There are several serological

types, but our main interest falls on the PMV group I, Newcastle disease.

Clinical signs can be summarized as follows: sudden death with no prior clinical signs, or just some hours of apathy; diarrhea in the visceral acute form, anorexia, and cyanosis. We also have a respiratory form with nasal exudate, dyspnea, anorexia, and lethargy. These last two forms may occur simultaneously. Additionally, there is the chronic form, which affects the central nervous system, causing convulsions, tremors, dystonia, opisthotonos, and torticollis.

Incubation time varies from 4 to 25 days; healthy carrier birds may occur. No effective vaccines are available; there is no specific treatment.

Adenovirus

Birds of all ages are susceptible to this DNA virus, represented by several stereotypes and groups. It was first described in *Agapornis roseicollis* (W. Pendleton *et al.*), causing depression and greenish feces. Histopathological tests show acute necrotizing pancreatitis; enlargement of the duodenal loop was also observed. Feather loss may occur. There is no specific treatment.

Psittacine Beak and Feather Disease Syndrome (PBFD)

The disease produces a varied group of symptoms, mainly disorders of the integument. Its true agent remains unknown, but much research points to a viral involvement.

Progressive loss of feathers is the principal clinical sign. The remaining feathers are curled and deformed, and dystrophic follicles are widespread. Beak lesions accompany a change in color, progressive elongation, and development of fractures. Diarrhea, lethargy, anorexia, loss of weight, and death may occur. Also observed is a behavior change: an increase of aggressiveness toward other birds.

Despite several continuing research projects, very little is known on its physiopathology, and there is no cure so far. Some authors recommend euthanasia.

Parasites

Included here are those diseases caused both by external parasites—such as lice, mites, fleas, fies, etc.—and internal parasites—such as protozoa and helminths. Some of the external (ecto-) parasites are macroscopic, while others are microscopic, even affecting the respiratory tract. The main genera are: *Dermanyssus* (red mite); *Knemidokoptes* (*laevis*); *Procnemidokoptes*; *Syringophilus*; *Pterolichus*; *Analges*; *Dermatoglyphos*; *Epidermoptides*.

They can be almost totally eliminated by aerosol-spray pesticides based on pyrethroids. Ivermectin can also be used orally 0.2 mg/kg, or I.M.

Intestinal Parasites:

Protozoa: *Trichomonas*, *Giardia*, *Eimeria*, and *Isospora*. In general, they cause diarrhea, anorexia, loss of weight, and several other

PBFDS in *roseicollis.* The affected birds become quite aggressive toward other birds and man.

A. roseicollis with PBFDS. Note the characteristic curled feathers. These birds become extremely aggressive towards other birds and also people.

symptoms. *Eimeria* and *Isospora* are agents of coccidiosis and enterorragia.

Helminths:

Ascaridia, *Spiroptera*, *Dispharynx*, and several cestodes. There are clinical signs specific to each parasite, but in general we find loss of weight and adinamia.

The following are some of the most common drugs used in the treatment of protozoa:

Metronidazole: 5 mg/kg, orally, every 8 hours.

Tinidazole: 5 mg/kg, orally, a single dose.

For helminths:

Albendazole: 12 mg/kg, orally, a single dose.

Mebendazole: 20 mg/kg, orally, a single dose, repeated after 10 days.

Thiabendazole: 200 mg/kg, orally, once a day for 3 days; repeat after 15 days.

Several others diseases and problems that affect the species exist, making it impossible to cover them all here. Nevertheless, there remains common problem that affects female birds and deserves our attention.

Egg Binding

Egg binding is not rare; and if not promptly treated, it can cause the female's death. It seems to be more prevalent in young females and in those susceptible to stress, which may be associated with sickness and overproduction.

The female must be assisted promptly in order to avoid death. A common procedure is to carefully aspirate the egg's content through the cloaca, while facilitating collapse of the shell by gentle palpation. This should be done very carefully and only by experienced persons.

Since most of the time a warm enema of vegetable oil is enough to solve the problem, this should be tried first. Oxytocin or ergonovine can also be used. The environmental temperature must be increased to 90° F. Antibiotics and multivitamins should also be administred.

Some cases will require that surgical procedures be employed; this should be attempted only by trained personnel. Recurrence of egg binding is not uncommon.

Often the first signs of PBFDS is a loss of feathers around the ears.

Cobalt Danish Violet (Violet Medium Pastel) back view. The interaction between one dark factor and one Danish Violet factor show us a stronger Violet shade.

APPENDIX 1: MUTATIONS IN THE GENUS *AGAPORNIS*

The factors found in lovebirds are listed by species. The symbols for both the normal and the mutant alleles are followed by an abbreviation indicating the mode of inheritance, as follows: AR: autosomal recessive; AC: autosomal codominant or incompletely dominant; SLR: sex-linked recessive; AD: autosomal dominant.

In the case of some mutations, the mode of inheritance shown here is only a conjecture, awaiting further research; these factors are marked with an asterisk (*).

MASKED LOVEBIRD, *A. PERSONATA*

Factor	*Normal Allele*	*Mutant Allele*	*Mode of Inheritance*
Blue	*A*	*a*	AR
Dilute	*D*	*d*	AR
Ino	*I*	*i*	AR
Dark	*e*	*E*	AC
Fallow	*F*	*f*	AR
Cinnamon*	*C*	*c*	SLR
Pied*	*p*	*P*	AD

FISCHER'S LOVEBIRD, *A. P. FISCHERI*

Factor	*Normal Allele*	*Mutant Allele*	*Mode of Inheritance*
Dilute	*D*	*d*	AR
Yellow	*Y*	*y*	AR
Blue	*A*	*a*	AR
Ino	*I*	*i*	AR
Golden	*g*	*G*	AD
Pied*	*P*	*p*	AR
Dark	*e*	*E*	AC
Lime	*G2*	*g2*	AR
Featherfooted	*s*	*S*	AC
Greenwing	*W*	*w*	AR
Fallow	*F*	*f*	AR

PEACH-FACE LOVEBIRD, *A. ROSEICOLLIS*

Factor	*Normal Allele*	*Mutant Allele*	*Mode of Inheritance*
Pastel (Blue)	*Y*	*y*	AR
American Pied	*p*	*P*	AD
Dark	*e(1, 2, 3)*	*E(1, 2, 3)*	AC
American Yellow	*A*	*a*	AR
Graywing	*A*	*a2*	AR
Japanese Yellow	*J*	*j*	AR
American Ino	Z^I	Z^i	SLR
Australian Ino	Z^I	Z^{ia}	SLR
American Cinnamon	Z^C	Z^c	SLR
West German Fallow	*F*	*f*	AR
East German Fallow	*F2*	*f2*	AR
Danish Violet	*v*	*V*	AC
American Violet	*v2*	*V2*	AC
Australian Yellow	*Pr*	*pr*	AR
Whiteface	*W*	*w*	AR
Orangeface	*l*	*L*	AC
Red-suffusion	*S*	*s*	AR
Red-eye	*r*	*R*	AD
Gray	*G*	*g*	AR
Gray Pastel	*gp*	*Gp*	AD

APPENDIX 2: IDENTIFICATION OF *AGAPORNIS* CHICKS

A. roseicollis, 0–4 days old

Phenotype	*Eyes*	*Beak*	*Down*	*Skin*
Green	dark black	grayish orange	orangeish salmon	
Pastel	dark	black	gray	salmon
Pied Green	dark	yellowish	orange	pied
Green Amer. Yellow, gray wings	purple	ochre	orange ochreous	orange ochreous
Pastel Amer. Yellow, gray wings	purple	ochre	grayish white	orange ochreous
Green Japanese Yellow	purple	light ochre	orange yellow	yellowish ochre
Pastel Japanese Yellow	purple	light ochre	white	yellowish ochre
Green Aus. Yellow	dark	light ochre	orange yellow	yellowish white
Pastel Aus. Yellow	dark	light ochre	white	yellowish white
Lutino	red	ochre	dark yellow	yellowish salmon
Creamino	red	ochre	dull white	yellowish salmon
Green Aus. Ino	rose	ochre	grayish yellow	yellowish salmon
Pastel Aus. Ino	rose	ochre	grayish ochre	yellowish salmon
Green Amer. Cinnamon	rose	brownish ochre	brownish orange	salmon
Pastel Amer. Cinnamon	light rose	dark ochre	grayish	salmon
Green Fallow	red	light ochre	light brownish orange	brownish salmon
Pastel Fallow	red	light ochre	yellowish white	brownish salmon
Green Orangeface	dark	grayish black	orangc	light orange
Pastel Orangeface	dark	grayish black	yellowish gray	yellowish salmon
Whiteface	dark	grayish black	bluish white	light salmon
Green Danish Violet	dark	black	bright bluish gray	grayish salmon
Pastel Danish Violet	dark	black	bright bluish gray	grayish salmon

Dark factor—has no specific pattern; it causes the darkening of the color tone colors with which it is combined, in proportion to the number of genes involved.

Other combinations will show intermediate color tones; sometimes it is very difficult to distinguish them in immature plumages.

APPENDIX 2: IDENTIFICATION OF *AGAPORNIS* CHICKS

A. personata forms, 0–4 days old

Phenotype	*Eyes*	*Beak*	*Down*	*Skin*
Green	dark	reddish orange	yellowish orange	salmon
Blue	dark	yellowish white	light gray	salmon
Lutino	red	orange	yellowish orange	pink
Albino	red	rose	white	pink

Dilute factor—lightens the above color tones.

Dark factor—darkens the above color tones.

BIBLIOGRAPHY

Almy, B. 1987. Some New Thoughts on Red-Suffusion. *Agapornis World*, 13-37, 19.

Aranyossy, P. 1985. Agaporniden Vertragen Keinen Frost. *AGA Rundbrief*ö1.

Arends, S. 1988. The Mysterious Dark Factor. *Agapornis World*, Vol. 14, No. 3.

Bates, H. and R. Busenbark. 1960. *Perroquets et Grandes Perruches*. Belgium: T.F.H. Publications. [Translation of *Parrots and Related Birds*.]

Bielfeld, H. 1982. *Handbook of Lovebirds*. Neptune, NJ: T.F.H. Publications.

Bloom, S. E. Current Knowledge about the W Chromosome. *Bioscience* 24, 340-344.

Brockmann, J. 1984. Gibt es doppelfaktorige Schekem beim Rosenköpfchen? *AGA Rundbrief*.

Brockmann, J. 1984. Vererbung der Lutino Schwarzköpfchen (*A. p. ?*), un einige Gedanken zum Thema "Verdacht Spaltvögel." *AGA Rundbrief*.

Brockmann, J. 1985. Blaue "Pfirsichköpfchen"—Amerkungen zur Vererbung. *AGA Rundbrief*ö5.

Brockmann, J. and W. Lantermann. 1985. *Agaporniden*, 2nd ed. Stuttgart: Verlag Eugen Ulmer. [In English as *The World of Lovebirds*, T.F.H. Publications.]

Brush, A. H. and H. Seifried. 1968. Pigmentation and Feather Structure in Genetic Variants of Gouldian Finch, *Poephila gouldiae*. *Auk* 85, 416-430.

Buckley, P. A. 1969. Disruption of Species-typical Behaviour Patterns in F1 Hybrid *Agapornis* parrots. *Tierpsychology* 26, 737-743.

Buckley, P. A. and F. Cooke. 1987. Avian Genetics, a Populational and Ecological Approach. London: Academic Press.

D'Angieri, A. 1982. Alguns aspectos do comportamento e genética dos *Agapornis*. *Ciência e Cultura*, Vol. 43, No. 11.

D'Angieri, A. 1984. Contribuições para o conhecimento do comportamento e genética the *Nymphicus hollandicus*. *Ciência e Cultura*, Vol. 36, No. 5.

D'Angieri, A. 1987. *Roseicollis* Ino Factor's Australian Allele. *Agapornis World*, Dec. 1987.

D'Angieri, A. 1988. *Agapornis?* Cuidados com suas espécies e mutações. Brasil: *Revista C.O.N.*.

D'Angieri, A. 1988. Intergeneric hybridization and inheritance of characters between *Penelope* and *Pipile*. *Mem. II International Symposium Cracidae*. Caracas: Universitat Simon Bolivar.

D'Angieri, A. 1989. *Agapornis* e suas mutações, introdução a genética. Brasil: *Revista C.O.N.*.

D'Angieri, A. and L. M. Oliveira. 1989a. Psittacin Absence in *roseicollis*, White-faced and Dutch Blue Inheritance Mechanism. *Agapornis World*, Sep. 1989.

D'Angieri, A. and L. M. Oliveira. 1989b. Structural Characters in *roseicollis*: "D" complex and Violet Factor. *Agapornis World*, Nov.-Dec. 1989.

Dilger, W. C. 1962. The Behaviour of Lovebirds. *Scient. Am.* 206, 88-98.

Edwards, J. 1960. The Simulation of Mendelism. *Acta genetica* 10, 63-70.

Forshaw, J. M. and W. T. Cooper. 1977. Parrots of the World. England: D&C.

Harrison, C. J. O. 1963. Non-melanic, Carotenistic and Allied Variant Plumages in Birds. *Bull. Br. Orn. Club.* 83, 90-96.

Harrison & Harrison. 1986. Clinical Avian Medicine and Surgery. Philadelphia: W. B. Saunders.

Hirai, K., S. B. Hitchner, and B. W. Calnek. 1979. Characterization of Paramyxo-herpes and Orbiviruses Isolated from Psittacine Birds. *Avian Dis.* 23, 148-163.

Hayward, J. 1987. Lovebirds and Their Colour Mutations. Poole, Dorset: Blandford Press.

Herröder, E. 1986. Besser für die Zücht: Flug oder Käfig? *AGA Rundbriefä*6.

Kathmann, F. 1985. Zuchtversuch für *Agapornis personata fischeri* in "Blau." *AGA Rundbriefü*9.

Kloosterman, J. 1987. *Roseicollis* and its Mutations—the Violet Character. *Agapornis World*, 1987.

Krammer, P. 1984. Gelbgeschekte Schwarzköpfchen (*A. p. personata*), Mutation oder Modifikation? *AGA Rundbriefö*5.

Lemster, Dirk. 1986. *Agapornis personata personata* und *p. fischeri* im Farbschlag Lutino? *AGA Rundbriefö*2.

Malachlan, G. R. and R. Liversidge. 1978. *Roberts' Birds of South Africa.* Capetown: Cape Transvaal Pub.

Morel, G. J., W. Gerle, and W. Haetwig. 1977. *A Field Guide to the Birds of West Africa.* London: Collins.

Ochs, B. 1984. Wildfarbige Schwarzköpfchen mit orangener Brust. *AGA Rundbriefö*6.

Ochs, B. 1985. Blaue Fischeri. *AGA Rundbriefö*5.

Roders, P. E. 1984. Aspergillose eine Schimmelpilzkrakheit. *AGA Rundbriefö*8.

Rollin, N. 1964. Non-hereditary and Hereditary Abnormal Plumage. *Bird Res.* 2, 1-44.

Ross, H. 1985. The Madagascar or Gray Headed Lovebird. *Agapornis Digest*, March 1985.

Schmidt, K. 1985. Die Zücht von Grauköpfchen. *AGA Rundbrief.*

Smith, W. R. 1937. Yellow Nyassas. *Australian Cage Bird Pub.*, May 29, 1937.

Smithe, F. B. 1978. *Naturalist's Color Guide.* New York: American Museum of Natural History.

Vaughan, J. 1987. The Violet Factor. *Agapornis Digest*, Sep. 1987.

Von Weyber and Van Wyk. 1987. The Black Eyed Yellow Fischer's Lovebird. *Agapornis World*, Vol. 13, No. 7.

Ziegenfuss, B. 1984. Russköpfchen—*Agapornis personata nigrigenis. AGA Rundbrief.*

INDEX

Page numbers in **boldface** refer to illustrations.